Professional English in Use

Management

Arthur McKeown
Ros Wright

CAMBRIDGE
UNIVERSITY PRESS

CAMBRIDGE UNIVERSITY PRESS
Cambridge, New York, Melbourne, Madrid, Cape Town,
Singapore, São Paulo, Delhi, Tokyo, Mexico City

Cambridge University Press
The Edinburgh Building, Cambridge CB2 8RU, UK

www.cambridge.org
Information on this title: www.cambridge.org/9780521176859

First published 2011

Printed in the United Kingdom at the University Press, Cambridge

A catalogue record for this publication is available from the British Library

ISBN 978-0-521-17685-9

Contents

Introduction

Who is this book for?

Professional English in Use Management is designed to help intermediate and upper intermediate learners of English to improve their management vocabulary – and perhaps even their knowledge of management. It is for people preparing to start studying for an MBA programme or a master's level course in management as well as for those already working in a management role who need English for their job.

You can use this book on your own for self-study, or with a teacher in the classroom, one-to-one or in groups.

How is this book organised?

The book has 40 two-page thematic units, in seven areas of management commonly studied on MBA courses worldwide: management in context, innovation, marketing, operations, people and human resources, finance and strategy and change.

The left-hand page of each unit presents new words and expressions in context in authentic texts, and the right-hand page allows you to check and develop your understanding of them through a series of different tasks.

There is an **answer key** at the back of the book. Most of the units have exercises with only one answer. However, some of the tasks, including the *Over to you* activities at the end of each unit (see opposite), are designed for writing and/or discussion about yourself and your own organisation, or one you would like to work for.

There is also an **index**. This lists all the words and expressions introduced in the book, and gives the unit numbers in which they appear. The index also tells you how the words and expressions are pronounced.

An **appendix** highlighting the difference between UK and US English terms can also be found at the end of the book.

The left-hand page

This page introduces new vocabulary for each thematic area in an authentic context, using the type of texts you will meet in MBA study and authentic business situations. The presentation is divided into sections indicated by letters – usually A, B and C – with simple, clear titles.

As well as explanations of vocabulary, there are examples of typical word combinations and the grammar associated with particular vocabulary, for example the verbs that are typically used with certain nouns.

The right-hand page

The tasks on the right-hand page give practice in using the new vocabulary presented on the left-hand page. Sometimes the tasks concentrate on using the words and expressions presented on the left-hand page in other business contexts. Other tasks test your understanding of the concepts on the left-hand page. Some units contain diagrams or tables to complete. As well as further explanations of the target vocabulary, there is information about typical word combinations, for example, the verbs that are typically used with certain nouns and the grammar associated with particular vocabulary items.

Over to you sections

An important feature of *Professional English in Use Management* is the **Over to you** section at the end of each unit. The **Over to you** sections give you the chance to explore the concepts and target vocabulary presented in the unit in relation to your own professional situation or studies. For some of these you will need to find information on the Internet.

Self-study learners can do this section as a written activity.

In the classroom, the *Over to you* sections can be used as the basis for discussion with the whole class, or in small groups with a spokesperson for each group summarizing the discussion and its outcome for rest of the class. The teacher can then get learners to look again at the exercises relating to points that have caused difficulty. Learners can follow up by using the *Over to you* section as a written activity, for example as homework, where appropriate.

How to use the book for self-study

Find the topic you are looking for by referring to the contents page or the index. Read through the texts on the left-hand page of the unit, and note the target vocabulary, which is marked in bold. Do the tasks on the right-hand page. Check your answers in the key. If you have made some mistakes, go back and look at the words in context and any explanations or definitions given in the texts or tasks again. In your notebook, note down important words and expressions and their meanings in the business context and also useful word combinations.

How to use the book in the classroom

The themes can be explored in the order given, so that the students' understanding develops from basic management concepts to more complex ones. Alternatively, teachers can choose units that relate to learner's particular needs and interests, for example areas they have covered in course books, or that have come up in other contexts. Alternatively, lessons can contain a regular vocabulary slot, where learners look systematically at the vocabulary of particular thematic areas.

Learners can work on the units in pairs, with the teacher going round the class assisting and advising. Teachers should get learners to think about the reasons why one answer is possible, and others are not.

We very much hope you enjoy using *Professional English in Use Management*.

1 Perspectives on management

A What is managing?

Consider several managers and their work.

> My job is simple: I have to make sure that the company finds customers in various sectors of the construction **industry**, **meets our production targets** and **makes a profit**.

Tom is the general manager of a brick company.

> Each season we create an innovative programme that will appeal to a broad range of audiences. We have **to set** realistic **prices** for tickets for each concert. We have to **cover our costs** within an **agreed annual budget**.

Harriet is the Chief Executive of a national orchestra.

> My job is to **pay attention to** every **detail** of every guest's stay with us.

Dick manages a major hotel

They all work in different environments, with different **stakeholders**, that is, all the people who can be affected by their company's actions, and different **key performance indicators** to **measure success**, but they share some general management responsibilities:

- **Identifying** customers' **needs**
- **Setting targets** and putting the necessary resources in place
- Planning and scheduling their own work and the team they manage
- Measuring performance and the outcomes achieved
- **Reporting on results.**

B Mintzberg

Henry Mintzberg, a Canadian professor of management, has made significant contributions to our understanding of **managerial work** and the role of the manager. He has identified different roles in a manager's job and placed them in three categories:

- *Interpersonal* roles – a manager is the **figurehead**, providing **leadership** for the team, the department or the organization and **liaising** with other stakeholders (both internal and external)
- *Information* roles – a manager has to be an **effective communicator** as information constantly moves in, round and out of the organization
- *Decision* roles – a manager has responsibility for **spotting opportunities**, **allocating resources** and **dealing with conflict** or the day-to-day differences that can arise in any team or organization.

C Management practice

Pavel is speaking to some new recruits at a major firm of management consultants, where he is to be their mentor during the first six months:

'Welcome to Delboi! I have three pieces of advice as you make the move from studying management to the real-world environment in which we work:

First: you need to be a **team player**. Our success here comes from **collaborating with colleagues** to create feasible solutions when we are **interacting with clients**.

Second: all the solutions that you recommend to our clients have to be practical rather than academic. You have to **integrate** what you have been learning and constantly **challenge your own assumptions**. You need to be able to **develop creative thinking skills** and **discuss complex issues** in the workplace from a 'people perspective'.

And finally: if you do not know something, or if you are uncertain about how we do things here, please ask!

'We hope you enjoy your time here and we look forward to working with you.'

1.1 Make ten word combinations from boxes 1 and 2. Look at A and B to help you.

1	allocate	cover	identify	make	measure	meet	pay attention to
	report on	set	spot				

2	a profit	costs	detail	needs	opportunities	performance
	prices	resources	results	targets		

1.2 Match one of Mintzberg's 10 Managerial Roles from the box with its definition below.

Disseminator	Disturbance handler	Entrepreneur	Figurehead	Leader
Liaiser	Monitor	Negotiator	Resource allocator	Spokesperson

Performing symbolic duties as a representative of the organization. ....

Collecting all types of information that are relevant and useful to the organization. ....

Developing and maintaining business networks. ....

Spotting opportunities, being innovative and championing change in products, services or business processes. ....

Dealing with unexpected challenges and crises. ....

Negotiating with individuals and dealing with other organizations. ....

Communicating information from inside the organization to outsiders. ....

Deciding on the most appropriate use of the organization's resources. ....

Communicating information from outside the organization to relevant groups inside the organization. ....

Establishing the organizational culture and motivating the staff. ....

1.3 Complete these testimonials from alumni students from an MBA programme using words or expressions from A, B or C.

1 Being able to make a p_____ is really only a tiny aspect of business. I_____ with experts from the various fields of management as well as c_____ with other students taught me to challenge my a_____s of the role of management. Amongst other things, the course gave me a practical insight into soft management skills as well as helping to d_____ my creative t_____ skills.

2 I now have a better idea about m_____ work in general. As a marketing manager, I was able to i_____ my previous experience with marketing. In addition, d_____ of the more c_____ i_____s of psychology during the course means that I am now much better at i_____ and meeting the n_____s of my customers. I also learnt how to become a much more effective c_____.

3 The part time Executive Programme gave me the chance to put the theory into practice immediately. I am responsible for s_____ and m_____ production targets for a small electronics firm. I learnt about the different management r_____ . This knowledge has made it easier for me to stick to an agreed b_____ for production and to apply key performance i_____ to monitor performance more accurately.

4 Not only did I learn how to become a team p_____, but I was able to develop my own personal l_____ skills. And by the end I had become a much more effective c_____. I'm far from becoming a f_____, but I do have much more confidence and have applied for management jobs in several different s_____ of i_____. I hope that soon I'll be able to m_____ a junior member of staff and put it all into practice.

Over to you

Look at Mintzberg's ten managerial roles in 1.2. Which ones do you identify in your current job or in a job you would like to have in the future? Why?

2 Organization structures

A Organizational structures

Management structures identify the different departments in an organization and set out who answers to whom in the **chain of command**.

The traditional types of organizational structure are **functional** or **divisional**. In a **functional structure**, the organization is divided up into different functional areas or departments, such as Marketing, Finance and Production. **Multi-divisional** structures also exist, where the organization is divided along **geographical** or **product divisions**. This allows the company to grow and develop in new parts of the world and to add new combinations of products. A multi-divisional **matrix** may also be adopted. This is a combination of **product** and **geographical divisions** that allows a large company to adapt products for particular markets.

Matrix structures are especially used in large organizations that have a number of clearly defined projects. Organizations with one single owner, a **sole trader**, often have **no formal structure**.

Large organizations may have a **tall structure**, with **complex hierarchies** and many **layers of management**, but even a very large organization can have a **flat structure**, with only a few levels of management.

An **organization chart** is a diagram showing relationships between different jobs and departments. It may identify the various **functional departments**, the hierarchy, from the **CEO** and the **Board of Management** downwards, and the **lines of responsibility**, to identify reporting channels (including individual managers' **spans of control**).

B An example of a divisional structure

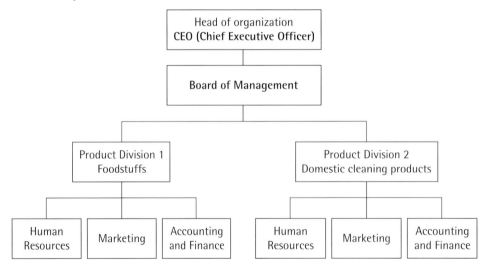

2.1 Match the terms in the box below with their definitions, using information from A and B.

chain of command	lines of responsibility	spans of control	Board of Management

1 Handing decision making from the higher levels of an organization to lower ones. ....

2 The number of people a manager can effectively manage in a particular situation. ....

3 The specification of individual employees' responsibilities for particular aspects of work and of their management responsibilities and who they report to in the organization. ....

4 A committee of members elected by the shareholders to manage and oversee the company. ....

2.2 Give each sentence below a subheading from the box.

flat	functional	matrix
multi-divisional	no formal structure	product

1 .... – departments are separated according to the different aspects of company work, such as producing goods or dealing with the financial matters.

2 .... – the company is divided into separate units specializing in a particular area of the world or has separate units dealing with particular types of products.

3 .... – the company uses a mixture of divisional structures, to enable it to be more flexible and organize its work around specific projects.

4 .... – very small companies run by a single person or group are like this.

5 .... – in this type of structure responsibility is shared, with fewer managers and with individuals being responsible for their own tasks.

6 .... – the organization is divided according to a particular product or type of product, each of which has functional teams to take care of staff, finance, etc.

2.3 Add words from the box into the correct phrase to make noun phrases.

command	control	management	responsibility

1 chain   of   ....

2 layer   of   ....

3 line   of   ....

4 span   of   ....

Over to you

Draw an organization structure for an organization with which you are familiar.

3 Some management gurus

A Henri Fayol (1841–1925)

Henri Fayol began his career as a mining engineer in Comentry-Fourchamboult-Decazeville, France. He was appointed director of a group of mines in 1872 and became managing director in 1888, before retiring in 1918.

His book *General and Industrial Management* demonstrates how general **management concepts** can be applied across a vast range of organizations, regardless of sector: **manufacturing**, **services**, **public sector**, etc. There are multiple layers to a manager's role, including having to develop a workable structure, dealing with staff – **roles and responsibilities**, as well as from a **motivational** perspective – considering the **macro environment** – that is the wider economic conditions that affect an organization, and drawing up a suitable **strategic plan**. Fayol also identified the major functions of '**administrative management**', such as marketing, production and finance.

B Frederick Winslow Taylor (1856–1915)

Frederick Winslow Taylor, an American engineer, is credited with being the inventor of '**scientific management**' in manufacturing environments.

As a manager at the Midvale Steel Works in Philadelphia he used a stopwatch and notebook to identify each step in the various **processes** on the factory floor. From these observations he was able to measure the **productivity rates** of workers at every stage in the different tasks he saw performed. He was then able to make recommendations that led to **greater efficiency** in the **production process**.

Taylor's *The Principles of Scientific Management*, published in 1911, was the first bestseller in the history of modern management. His work had a huge impact on how factories were managed in the early decades of the twentieth century, especially in America and Europe. Henry Ford, for example, followed the principles of Taylorism, scientific management and **mass production** when he set up the Ford Motor Company in 1903. He introduced the Model T Ford in 1909 and soon **captured** a huge **share of the** American car **market**: in 1918, fifty per cent of all the cars on American roads were Model T Fords. In the Soviet Union, Lenin urged workers to use **production targets** that followed the **principles of Taylorism**; failure to do so could lead to severe penalties and punishment.

C Peter Drucker (1909–2005)

Peter Drucker is regarded by many of his peers as the most significant **management guru** of modern management practice.

Drucker was born in Austria in 1909. He moved to America, via England, in 1937 and worked at General Motors as a **management consultant** during the Second World War. His academic career began after the war.

The focus of his work, and a major reason for his appeal to practising managers, is on the practical application of **management theories** to the real-world working environments in which managers do their jobs and seek to achieve results. That said, ideas such as **management by objectives**, **decentralization** and **knowledge working** can all be traced back to Drucker's work, many years before they entered mainstream management thinking.

His **seminal work** 'What Makes an Effective Executive?' in 2004 was awarded the McKinsey Prize for the best *Harvard Business Review* article of the year.

3.1 Find seven word combinations using **management** from A, B and C. Then match five of them to the correct definition below.

    1 A person with knowledge or expertise who becomes an intellectual guide for others in a particular aspect of the field.

    2 Someone who advises people on management issues for a fee.

    3 The rationalization and standardization of work through division of labour, time and motion studies, work measurement, and piece-rate wages, as defined by US engineer, Frederick Winslow Taylor.

    4 An idea or principle connected with something abstract concerning management.

    5 Related to businesses' managerial roles and administrative functions, as defined by French engineer, Henri Fayol.

3.2 Complete the PowerPoint slide using information from A.

Managers must/need to...

    1 examine the organization's .... environment and draw up .... plans for the organization's response to what is likely to lie ahead.

    2 build up the .... plan of the organization and put in place procedures which can help with the preparation and implementation of plans.

    3 .... and set an example for their staff, as well as clarify the .... and .... of the organization's teams and individuals.

    4 ensure that the work done by the various teams and departments is consistent with the overall plan for the organization.

    5 ensure that what happens is what should happen, in accordance with the organizational plan.

3.3 Complete the statements and then decide to which management guru, Fayol, Taylor or Drucker, each one is attributed. Use words and expressions from A, B and C.

    1 Production .... at the turn of the twentieth century across Europe and the USA benefited greatly from the .... of the .... theory of management, based on research into .... production which dealt with optimum .... rates and resulted overall in greater .... Production .... were set for individuals according to the time available and the share of the workload. Applying these principles enabled Ford to .... the major share of the automobile market at the beginning of the twentieth century. The man who developed these theories was ....

    2 .... are those who develop and use knowledge in the workplace. Along with the .... of the role of management, these are just two of the concepts that can be attributed to one person in particular, ...

    3 The manufacturing and .... industries as well as the .... sector have gained from a greater understanding of the roles of management, and the separate functions involved in management, as highlighted in the .... work of ....

Over to you

Explore the profiles of the major management gurus, especially those mentioned in other units in this book, available at www.thinkers50.com

4 Management in different sectors

A Private

Hong works for a large hotel chain in Guangzhou, China. She is in charge of a customer service team:

'The company is under **private ownership**. Our founder was an **entrepreneur** who spotted an opportunity to provide high-quality conference facilities for the growing number of trade shows and industrial exhibitions attracted to the region. Part of the **equity** is still in the hands of the family; a minority of the shares is held by a number of **institutional investors**.

'We also have **strategic partnerships** with local, national and international airlines and tour operators.

'In all that we do our mission is strictly commercial; we have to **generate a profit** for the family and for the **institutional shareholders**.

'The customer service team works closely with managers and staff in every part of the customer experience, so that every guest receives an excellent level of service at each stage of their stay with us. The company operates within a very **competitive business**. If we don't keep our customers satisfied we won't survive.'

B Public

Jo is a public sector employee working for the City Council in Madison, Wisconsin. She is a food safety officer, with responsibility for a team of ten food safety inspectors:

'Our **mission** is simple: we exist to serve the public by ensuring that health is not put at risk by unsafe food. This mission is then developed into a series of **strategic** and **operational plans** that are discussed and approved each year by the council's senior management team.

'Members of the team make regular visits to restaurants and other places where food is prepared and sold to the public. We also visit food-processing factories to monitor standards like cleanliness, general hygiene and cold storage.

'We are not **profit seeking**, rather, we have to make sure we can provide services within the budget agreed and endorsed for each year.

'My own job involves:

- **planning** and **scheduling** the work done by the members of the team
- ensuring that adequate **resources** are in place to support their work
- monitoring the regular inspections (including any recommendations for **preventative** and **corrective action** required) so that I can provide regular reports to my own line manager.'

C Not for Profit

David manages the furniture workshop in a social enterprise in Dublin, Ireland:

'A social enterprise is a business with primarily **social objectives**, so we do not focus on making a profit from our activities. Any **financial surplus** we can generate is re-invested in the business or in the community. We do not have to maximize profits for owners or **shareholders**.

'There are many different kinds of social enterprise but they are all **accountable to** their **stakeholders** such as employees, clients, local community groups or other users.

'Our mission is to make life better in this community by creating income and employment for local people. We do this by taking in **donations** of furniture, repair it if necessary and clean it for resale to our customers.

Like other **non-profit organizations**, we have a **triple bottom line**:

- we minimize any negative effects on the environment
- we have to be aware of the needs of our staff, both **waged** and **volunteers**
- we have to make enough profit or surplus to provide a **sustainable business**.

It is never easy to balance all three of these but it is very **satisfying work**.'

4.1 Change the nouns in the box into adjectives.

competition/competitor	correction	entrepreneur	finance	institution
privacy	public	society	strategy	sustainability

4.2 Using expressions from the texts on the left, match the questions (1–6) and answers (a–f) following an MBA lecturer's session.

1 I was just wondering, Dr Khomer, if you could clarify the meaning of public sector?
2 Dr Khomer, You mentioned something about social objectives, but I didn't quite catch what you said ...
3 Excuse me, could you elaborate a little on what you meant by the term sustainable business?
4 Yes, Dr Khomer, I just wondered what you had to say about institutional investors.
5 Sorry, I didn't quite understand your point about financial surplus. Could you show us the slide again please?
6 Yes, I'd like to know what you mean by triple bottom line exactly.

a They include the production and supply of quality goods and services, adoption of fair-trade practices and contribution to the general welfare of society.
b These consist of entities, such as pension funds, insurance companies and investment banks, with large amounts to invest.
c Yes, it refers to the generation of resources, such as capital that exceeds expenditure.
d Sure. It's an accounting term that means the most important factors for measuring an organization's success in social and environmental as well as economic terms – we say people, planet, profit.
e The army is an example of an organization that provides a public service funded by the government.
f This refers to the need for an organization to make enough profit or surplus for it to survive.

4.3 Complete these observations from employees of three enterprises. Choose words from the box.

accountable	competitors	donate	equity	mission	non-profit
organization	planning	profit	resources	satisfying	shareholders
social	volunteer	waged			

1 We don't hold e.................... and so our m.................... as a s.................... enterprise is to generate financial r.................... to facilitate the operation of our association.
2 P.................... a schedule for the v.................... who run our n.................... is not a simple task; while we don't have a problem finding people willing to d.................... their time free of charge, they are not necessarily available when we need them. Luckily, we also have a group of w.................... staff working specific shifts to ensure a permanent presence. They all agree it's highly s.................... work.
3 Being a.................... to our s.................... is a necessary evil for any private enterprise. It is vital that we provide them with an annual report, outlining the amount of p.................... generated over each 12-month period, as well as our positioning compared to that of the current c.................... in the market.

Over to you

Find out more about Muhammad Yunus and the Grameen Bank. Compare and contrast his ideas with the principles on which private and public sector organizations are run.

5 Resources managers use

A Data and information

Roberto manages the loyalty card scheme for a large supermarket chain that rewards shoppers when they make purchases:

'We use computers running **proprietary software** to find patterns and trends in customers' purchasing habits. Reductions in storage costs and techniques for **data mining** let us **collect and analyse data** for every single purchase. This has brought significant changes in the way we can manage our stores throughout the country and elsewhere in our overseas branches. Most of our customers have loyalty cards. Every single **transaction** they make can be recorded and analysed using a **sophisticated database software package**. We are able to **access** huge **amounts of data** and by using elaborate **statistical techniques** we can analyse the **raw data** to identify significant factors and make predictions on a region-by-region and store-by-store basis.

This helps us make better informed decisions about:

- the amount of **shelf space** we allocate to different products in different stores
- stock, **inventory control** and reordering
- **logistics** for getting deliveries on time to each store.'

B Time

*Paul, the **senior partner** in a major firm of management consultants, is talking about how he and his colleagues charge their time to the client*:

'Like other providers of professional services, we use **time management software** to record time spent on the various projects we are involved in. This can include project preparation, face-to-face meetings with the client and any **work off-site**. We also charge for travel and accommodation, plus any other **incidental expenditure**.

All of this is set out in advance in our standard **terms of reference** for each individual project. This is **signed off** by both the client and us before work begins, so there are no nasty surprises when the bills start to arrive on the client's desk.

Of course, staff at different **grades** are charged out at different **daily rates**; the daily rate for a **junior consultant** is significantly lower than the rate for a senior partner. The **project manager** can easily compile regular **statements of account** and **invoices** by using data from the system.'

C Money

*Tim is the Director of Innovation in a university. He is talking to an MBA class about **sources of finance** for a **start-up business***:

'Money makes the business world go round; a manager, regardless of their role and the sector in which they work, has to understand some basic principles of finance. Starting a new business is exciting!

Let's think for a few minutes about where entrepreneurs can find **funding** for their new enterprise:

- **savings** are a possibility
- **grants**, for example from the Government
- **loans** from family and friends; banks, who will want some form of **collateral** to protect their money
- firms of **venture capitalists** who are prepared to take a lot of risk in return for making a substantial profit
- individual **business angels**, bearing in mind they are interested in the equity and may even want to get directly involved in the business.'

5.1 Find seven noun phrases and three verb phrases using the words **data** and **software** from A and B.

5.2 Find words or word combinations in A with the following meanings.

1 Copyrighted computer programs developed and sold by a commercial IT company
2 The exchange of goods or services between buyer and seller for money
3 The management of business operations, such as the acquisition, storage, transportation and delivery of goods along the supply chains
4 Keeping track of goods or products available for purchase at a shop or warehouse at a particular moment in time usually via a software package
5 Goods or products held in a shop or warehouse
6 The area available in a shop to display stock for purchase

5.3 Suszanna responds to questions from Markus confirming the terms of reference for a new contract. Complete the dialogue, using B to help you. Then decide who is the project manager and who is the junior consultant.

Markus: Sorry to disturb you, I'm trying to make sense of these terms. Could you just confirm a few things for me before I .... this contract? I know the daily .... depends on my .... but I'm not sure of the rest.

Suszanna: Well, basically, the .... of .... are set out by our company, as the consultancy firm, and you can use our .... management .... to keep track of the hours you do.

Markus: OK, I understand. What if I'm working ....; what am I entitled to?

Suszanna: The usual, accommodation and travel but also any incidental ...., such as internet fees and photocopying. So make sure you keep all your receipts.

Markus: I'm sure I'll lose some of them from time to time. Do I need to send .... to the clients?

Suszanna: No. Send them to me and I'll download a .... of .... and the invoices and send them to the client for payment.

5.4 Complete the explanations using the correct terms and expressions from C.

1 Family and friends can always be of help by providing .... for a .... business. Stelios Haji-Ionanou, for example, had access to $20 million in funding, thanks to his family's shipping business. This is how he was able to fund the loan to set up EasyJet, a major European low-cost airline.
2 .... may be available in some areas to encourage innovation and to attract inward investment. Local enterprise agencies will be able to help you to identify these potential .... of finance and to discuss the criteria for eligibility.
3 Unlike grants, ... have to be paid back. It is worth trying different banks and finance houses to find out what is available. Lenders will normally require some form of .... such as property, as a guarantee that the borrower will pay back the loan.
4 If you're lucky, you may be able to identify ....: people who will help to fund the business, usually in return for a share of the business or its profits.'
5 Then there's .... capital – this is another source of private equity. Providers are seeking to invest other people's money and expect their investment to have paid off within seven years.
6 Finally, if none of these options is available, entrepreneurs may even consider using their own private .... to fund a small business venture.

Over to you

Webquest: use your online searching skills to find out more about career opportunities in management consultancy. Write a mini-report about a job that interests you.

6 Innovation and creativity

A

Sources of innovation

Organizations of every sort need to **innovate** if they are to survive and thrive. This may involve developing new products or services, improving existing products or services, or making changes to existing working practices or procedures.

Managers need to challenge the **status quo** in regular reviews of **trends** and changes in the macro-environment, and to seek better alternatives to their organization's products, services and operational processes. This may often require **taking risks** and clearly specifying the **benefits** expected from the innovation.

Innovation is different from **invention**: inventions are often the result of an individual's **ingenuity** in creating a new product idea, whereas innovation generally involves a team working together to develop business solutions and significant **competitive advantage** for their organization.

Innovation is also different from **creativity**: creativity involves thinking of novel and appropriate ideas, whereas innovation is the process by which ideas are turned into practice or product.

Innovation consists of distinct stages:

- *Idea generation* – the development of a **design concept** or **technical proposal** by integrating market needs with technical information
- *Problem solving* – R&D (**research and development**) and engineering to develop a technical solution to the proposal
- *Implementation and diffusion* – market introduction, and the communication and use by which the innovation comes to have a wider social and economic impact.

Innovation and new ideas can come from within a manager's team, from elsewhere in the organization, or from customers, suppliers and other stakeholders. **Consumers** play two roles:

- as a resource to supply customer-need information and to evaluate ideas for new products
- as a **co-creator** where customers collaborate and participate actively in the development and testing of the **viability** of an **initial concept**.

Lead users are customers who are well ahead of **market trends**, and who **have a propensity** to innovate solutions to their own problems. Marketers often look to lead users for useful insights for innovations and possibly even **commercialize** their innovations for other customers.

B

Trevor Baylis: a case study on the value of market research in the innovation process 1

Trevor Baylis, the British inventor of the clockwork radio, had his **'a-ha' moment** when he saw an opportunity to develop a radio that uses a simple clockwork mechanism rather than batteries. He created a **prototype** that was **market tested** in rural South Africa with **potential customers**. Further **product development** was carried out in Britain to increase its robustness and functionality before the product was **launched** onto market. Now, twenty years after the development of the initial concept, the product is well established. Lead users were large aid agencies, who purchased the radios in bulk to be used in areas hit by natural disasters, where the electricity and communications infrastructure has collapsed.

6.1 Steve talks about entrepreneurs he has known. Complete his thoughts using expressions from A. You may need to change the form of some words.

'The most important characteristic was the enthusiasm they brought to business.

1 They are good at spotting .... in the macro-environment and don't just accept the ....

2 Almost everyone takes .... and is prepared to gamble with their time, commitment and money.

3 They are flexible and willing to experiment with their .... to make it work.

4 They utilize their sense of .... to the benefit of the company and have a .... to know exactly when to ....

5 All of them recognize the need to .... their innovative product or service and ultimately achieve competitive ....'

6.2 Match the words and expressions (1–9) to the correct definition (a–i). Use A and B to help you.

1	'a-ha' moment	a	to introduce a new product to the market
2	to launch	b	a product sample used to get feedback from likely customers
3	viability	c	a new product or service designed from someone's idea
4	to test a market	d	the ability to succeed over the long term
5	prototype	e	the time when an entrepreneur gets a new idea
6	ingenuity	f	those likely to be interested in a product or service
7	invention	g	the skill of inventing new things
8	potential customers	h	document that identifies the technical requirements of a project or product and explains a plan to meet them
9	technical proposal	i	to explore the reaction of the buyer to a new product or service

6.3 Use the words in the box to complete the banner for this homepage.

co-creator	competitive	concept	consumer	development	innovation (x2)
product	research	trends			

Essential to the success of any industry is .... pushes the boundaries in .... development enabling companies to gain that all-important .... advantage. The *2011 Innovation Awards for Industrial Design* recognize individuals with proven expertise in .... and .... who have come up with a design .... that responds to current market .... in the field of industrial design. The difference with this year's winner – he or she will have worked directly with the .... as .... to come up with the winning concept.

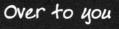

Over to you

What do you think is more important for an organization, to be able to develop creative ideas or to be innovative and turn creative ideas into practice?

7 Screening ideas

A Criteria for screening ideas

Dr Brown is talking about the importance of using clear criteria in making decisions for selecting and screening new ideas:

It is important to have a structured approach and transparent **consultation process** for selecting the best ideas for further research and development. Companies typically establish **screening criteria** to provide an **objective** procedure for **evaluating the potential** of ideas for new products. This reduces **subjectivity** and provides a unity of purpose and a context for our new product planners.

Screening criteria usually involve three factors:

1 *Market criteria* – market size and the product's attractiveness to a range of customers; market share and the percentage of the market we can get; likely trends in market growth; market positioning and **differentiation** – how it is different from competitors' products; ease of **distribution**

2 *Product criteria* – newness: will it have some novelty? Technical feasibility: can we actually make it? Compatibility: does it fit in with other products in our **product portfolio** – that is, the full range of products we sell?

3 *Financial criteria* – sales value and profitability; return on investment; cash flow.

We use a simple **checklist** in a **decision-making grid** to ensure we do not omit or overlook **key criteria**. Usually, three ideas are discussed in departmental meetings in which we **brainstorm** and develop them and make decisions about any further development work that might be required.

This is the table we use in my team to screen new ideas:

Criteria		Idea 1	Idea 2	Idea 3
Must-have criteria	Does it fill a perceived need?			
	Does it have **unique product characteristics** that offer distinctive benefits to the user?			
	Will it make sufficient contribution to profit?			
	Is it saleable in large, expanding territories?			
Would-like criteria	Does it fit in with our product portfolio?			
	Is it suitable for **mass media advertising** and **promotion**?			

B Trevor Baylis: a case study on the value of market research in the innovation process 2

Christopher Staines, a colleague of Trevor Baylis, talks about the development of the clockwork radio technology:

'When I met Trevor we had a lot of work to do to protect the intellectual property in his idea and we had to ensure that the basic idea was technically feasible for mass production.

We also had to consider significant **commercial realities**:

■ Is there a real need for the product?

■ Can we make it?

■ Will people buy it, at a price where we can make money?

Now, twenty years after its development, the **original concept** has been **modified** and extended for use in clockwork radios and chargers for mobile telephones.'

7.1 Find seven noun phrases from A using the word **criteria**.

7.2 Join the two halves of the sentences to create definitions of the words in the box.

brainstorming	checklist	objective	subjective

1	Based on personal beliefs, or opinions	a	to think aloud and suggest as many ideas as possible.
2	A set of important or relevant actions	b	rather than personal opinions.
3	A session where participants are encouraged	c	instead of on verifiable evidence.
4	Based on evidence and reason	d	or steps to be taken or criteria to be met.

7.3 Complete the interview with Tony Hsieh using expressions from A and B.

Soon after Tony Hsieh (pronounced Shay) joined Zappos at the age of 24, the company grew from almost no sales to over $1 billion annually. We asked him about the success of the company.

'We've been asked by a lot of people just how we grew so quickly, and the answer is actually really simple. A .... process and .... of the .... market led to our original concept, which was to provide the best customer service possible. For example, we have a unique .... policy that provides the benefit of free shipping both ways. Our customers will often buy ten pairs of shoes, select one pair they really like in the comfort of their own home and then return the other nine pairs to us.

We don't spend a lot of money on traditional means of .... through .... media. Instead, we try to .... just our service and enhance the customer experience so that we get a lot of repeat customers, many of whom switch brands from our competitors. Much to our surprise, the .... concept worked so well there was never any need to .... it. We produce shoes, there is nothing unique in the product ...., neither is our .... particularly extensive. However, what we did realise was that there were certain obvious commercial ....: everyone needs shoes, our prices are reasonable but still make a profit and, of course, we can do better than the competition!'

Over to you

Visit www.wackyinventions.com and select three inventions. Then devise your own decision-making grid to evaluate each invention. Use examples from your observation and experience to discuss how managers like Tony Hsieh can innovate by challenging the status quo.

8 Feasibility studies

A The new product development process

The **new product development process** uses a series of stages and gates. A **Stage-Gate Process** is a way of moving a **new-product project** from idea to launch. This is a carefully designed business process, based on comprehensive research into understanding product success and failure.

Stage-Gate divides the effort into distinct stages separated by management **decision gates**. At each stage **product champions** and developers must complete a prescribed set of related cross-functional tasks prior to obtaining management approval to proceed to the next stage.

Each stage represents a distinct set of related activities, normally grouped into five stages using **gate criteria**, as shown in the diagram below. At each stage an idea may be approved, rejected or sent for rework.

Product launch, also termed **new product introduction**, occurs at the end of the commercialization stage.

Following launch, the separate process of **product life-cycle** management begins.

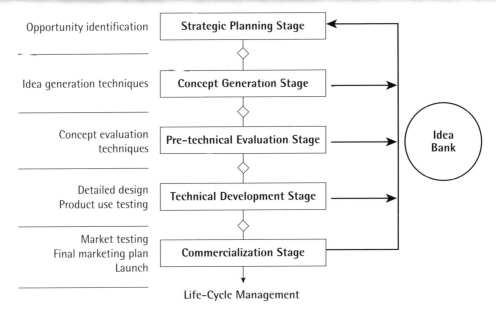

The new product development process

B Is there a need for a product or service?

When product design and market opportunities are complex, a preliminary investigation, called a **feasibility study**, will be conducted. This is the systematic and detailed assessment of whether a design, process or material for production fulfils all the **technical requirements**.

This must take place before detailed (and expensive!) **primary market research** is carried out so that a business case can be prepared to demonstrate that the project is worth developing further.

Evidence based on informal enquiries with current customers can be used at this stage. Any **quantitative data** (based on numbers, percentages and statistics) and **qualitative data** (based on attitudes, opinions and preferences) that can be gathered from existing **in-house sources** such as the **company's accounting system** or recent **sales records** can be valuable. There may be some **secondary market information** available in **government statistics** and in publications from relevant **industry bodies** or the local **chamber of commerce**.

More formal primary marketing research can be done later, involving **online surveys**, **focus groups** and **structured interviews** with those likely to be interested in the new product or service.

8.1 Find six word combinations using the word **product** from A.

8.2 Put the different stages of the Stage Gate process into the most appropriate order then add headings to the table, using terms from A. One is done for you.

		1. Strategic planning			
a A tangible prototype is created and evaluated using both market and technical criteria.	b Is it possible to deliver the new product technology?	c Is there evidence of market size and technical feasibility to create a market opportunity?	d Is there market interest in the product concept, market viability, revenue potential, etc?	e The product is finally put on the market.	f The product takes its ultimate form and marketing plans are evaluated.

8.3 Choose the correct definition of each of these noun phrases.

1 An industry body:
 a A professional group that oversees standards and represents the interests of manufacturers in a particular sector.
 b A government body that oversees the standards of industry in a particular sector.

2 A trade fair:
 a An event where manufacturers from one industry attempt to exchange their products and services with manufacturers from a different industry.
 b An event where manufacturers from a particular industry present their products and services to potential retailers and distributors.

3 A focus group
 a A group in a company who analyses its consumers and their needs.
 b Groups of consumers who evaluate a new product or service.

4 A Chamber of Commerce
 a An association of businesses in a local city or region which protects the economic interests of its members.
 b A building where businesses come to carry out their trade.

5 A trade journal
 a A periodical or magazine about international trade.
 b A periodical or magazine aimed at providing news and information for specialists in a particular area of business, e.g. motor manufacturing or petroleum engineering.

6 Product champion
 a An individual who recognizes a new technology or market opportunity as having significant potential and generates support from other people in the organization.
 b A best-selling product or product range.

Over to you

Search online using the key term *stage-gate process* to learn more about this process.

Give some examples of how you can map some real instances of new product development to the stage-gate diagram.

9 New product development in practice

A Diffusion of innovation and customer adoption of new products

Diffusion of innovation is the process by which new ideas, products and technology spread through a society or a culture.

The Everett Rogers framework describes the way consumers **evaluate** and **adopt** new products and the categories of consumers at **stages of adoption** as the product **diffuses** through the market.

Diffusion of an innovation occurs over a period of time among the members of a customer group, and involves the following stages: awareness, interest, evaluation, trial and adoption.

Rogers identifies five categories of adopters:

- *Innovators* – the first group to adopt a new product is a small group of individuals who are very open to new ideas and prepared to take a risk.
- *Early adopters* – the next people to adopt the product are often opinion leaders who serve as vital links to members of the early majority group.
- *Early majority* – this next group of adopters want to be sure that a new product will prove successful before they adopt it.
- *Late majority* – these are people who may be forced to adopt a new product for economic or social reasons.
- *Laggards* – often stubbornly resist change and are the last group to adopt the product.

B The Maclaren Baby Buggy

Owen Finlay Maclaren, a retired aeronautical **designer** and former test pilot, used his **aircraft design** experience in **designing** and manufacturing baby buggies. The Maclaren buggy's wheels and folding mechanism reflect its designer's specialist knowledge and experience of aeronautical engineering.

To Maclaren a baby buggy had to be durable, safe and lightweight; so he redesigned the pushchair from the **traditional design**. Maclaren's **design director** later commented: 'he solved a very difficult engineering problem. Today we are using **computer-aided design** systems to model solutions like that.'

He **secured investment** and the first buggy was sold in 1967. By the 1990s production had reached half a million a year, with steadily growing **order books** as **export sales** developed.

The development of balloon tyres, with rubber made to a **special formula**, to give babies a smoother ride was another 'first' for Maclaren.

Maclaren died in 1978, but his **vision** transformed baby transport all over the world. The **revolutionary design** liberated parents from the bulky pram and quickly became an **object of desire** for new parents. Maclaren Ltd today is a **highly successful business**, consistently winning **design and safety awards** for **a wide range of products**, all variations on the original theme.

C Some disasters

The Edsel was a brand of car manufactured by Ford in the late 1950s that became synonymous with **innovation failure**. There were several **contributory factors**:

- *The late '50s recession* – potential customers preferred a less **innovative product**.
- *The design* – service engineers found the engine difficult to work on.
- *The price* – the car was perceived as too expensive.
- At 84,000, total sales failed to meet the company's **projected break-even point** of 170,000 needed to make a profit.
- Fifty years after its **spectacular failure**, fewer than 6,000 Edsels now survive. Considered collectors items, they are highly desirable in the eyes of car enthusiasts.

9.1 Label the chart using terms from A, then complete the summary using these words: **adopt, diffuse, evaluate, innovate** and terms from A.

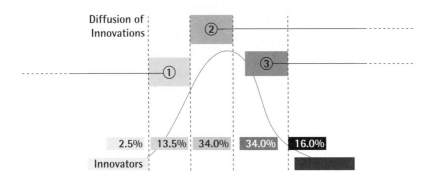

This curve shows the .... of an .... in the market as it is .... by groups of consumers over a period of time. It shows how very small groups of .... are the first to try out new ideas, which are then .... by other consumers. Some groups wait until the innovation is successful or until they need to own it. These are known as the .... and ...., respectively.

9.2 Use the words and expressions in the box to complete the text about entrepreneur Levi Roots.

export	highly successful business	order book	revolutionary
secret formula	secured investment	wide range of products	vision

After appearing in a TV programme for would-be entrepreneurs, successful reggae singer, Levi Roots has developed a .... business, selling *Reggae Reggae Sauces*, a range of hot spicy barbeque sauces and seasoning. Levi had a .... and soon .... in return for a substantial share of the equity in his company. Levi has gone on to win huge orders from major supermarket chains for his sauces, made to a .... based on an original recipe from his grandmother in the Caribbean. Retailers now stock a growing range of flavours; pack sizes as well as a growing .... This now .... will soon be stocking a .... And there are hopes of substantial .... sales in the near future.

9.3 Match the two halves of the sentences and put them into the correct part of the text.

1	Contributory factors leading	a	the latest object of desire,
2	enjoying huge success with the iPhone,	b	turn out innovation failures ...
3	only 42,000 Pippins were sold –	c	to such a spectacular failure included
4	even revolutionary designers, Apple	d	its projected break-even point barely met.

Despite ...., it seems that .... from time to time. Launched in 1996, the Bandai Pippin was Apple's effort to compete with the likes of Nintendo and Sony. Combining a networked computer with a home games console, Apple created the Pippin platform and hoped to license it to other companies. Bandai, looking for a way to get in to the games market, snapped it up. .... the fact that its library of games and software were poor in comparison with rival home consoles and it was reputed that ....

Over to you

Give some examples from your own observations or experience of how diffusion of innovation and the customer adoption model work in practice.

10 Intellectual property

A Patents

*Jon, a **patent attorney** based in Sydney, is outlining some key issues:*

'Coming up with a **killer idea** is by far the easiest part of the new product development process. Developing that **brainwave** into a successful product or service can be a minefield. There are several ways of protecting ideas, inventions and **intellectual property**:

- **Patents** can protect what products are made of and how things work.
- **Copyright** protects literary and artistic works, for example, books and pictures.
- **Trademarks** protect a brand of a company.

We generally ask clients to consider the following points before **taking out a patent**:

- It is essential that you get everyone involved to sign **non-disclosure agreements** before they receive any significant information about the proposed innovation.
- A **patent search** can be used, for a **small fee**, to find out if someone has already **patented your idea**; this should be done before you spend a lot of money on **developing a prototype** or carrying out expensive market research.
- You can make a **patent application**; you can use the term '**Patent Pending**' to describe your idea while the application is being processed.'

B Software piracy

As the Internet took off in the 1990s, games, software and music were often downloaded for free by users, especially teenagers, who did not see such activity as **theft**.

Shawn Fanning's Napster, an online music file-sharing service, allowed people to share their MP3 files with other users, thus bypassing the established market for such songs. The music industry **brought cases** in which they accused Fanning and his users of massive **copyright violations**. The service was issued a **court order**.

Spotify is a more recent example of a **legitimate** music file-sharing service. Users can get access to a mass catalogue of music of many different genres that can either be played on their computer (during which they receive occasional advertisements) or **ad-free**, in return for a small monthly **subscription**.

C Creative Commons

Creative Commons is a non-profit organization that seeks to increase the amount of creativity (cultural, educational and scientific content) in '**the commons**'; in other words, available to the public for free and **legal sharing** and use. Creative Commons provides free, easy-to-use legal tools to help everyone, from individual creators to large companies and institutions, with a simple way to **grant copyright permissions** to their **creative work**.

One organization that makes its content available **under a Creative Commons licence** is *OpenCourseWare*, which provides teaching materials.

10.1 Use the terms **Patents, Trademarks, Copyrights** to complete the explanations, using. A to help you.

.... protect material such as books, photographs, films, TV and music.

.... protect new inventions and cover how inventions work, allows exclusive rights to manufacture, use or sell an invention.

.... protect brand identities, symbols and logos that will distinguish an organization's products or services from those sold by another organization.

10.2 Find six word combinations using the word **patent**. Then match five to the correct definition.
1 An expert specializing in the legal aspects of innovation and new product development.
2 The act of obtaining protection for a new invention.
3 Carrying out research to ensure the new invention doesn't already exist.
4 Requesting protection for the new invention.
5 The term used while waiting for a patent to be granted.

10.3 Niki is talking about the innovation culture in her design company. Use the words and phrases in the box to complete her explanation.

brainwaves	copyright violation	creative work	develop prototypes
intellectual property	killer ideas	non-disclosure agreements	patent search
small fee			

'We are not short of .... or .... However, managers and senior staff have a significant role to play in seeking out opportunities for innovative ideas and in testing their feasibility. We can only survive and thrive if we all agree to work as follows:
- To protect the .... rights of any ideas or innovations in the .... that we do
- Where necessary, we need our partners and suppliers on individual projects to sign .... before significant work is done
- To .... of new products
- To agree to have a full-scale .... carried out
- To avoid any form of .... that could damage the reputation of the company.'

10.4 Complete this student's notes on intellectual property, using terms from A, B and C.

Wikipedia – the world's largest and most cited collaborative encyclopaedia is one example of content available under a .... By allowing people to .... share content, this has since become one of the greatest cultural resources of the digital revolution.

Flickr – the photo sharing site .... to the creative work of photographers around the world, enabling millions of photos to be in 'the ....'.

Over to you

Think about a product or service you know. What form of intellectual property protection do you think it would need, e.g. patent, trademark, copyright? To find out more, visit the 'Types of IP' section of the UK Intellectual Property Office website, www.ipo.gov.uk

11 Marketing principles

A Needs and wants

MBA teacher, Professor Smith, is introducing the overview of a module he is about to deliver in the new semester:

'The Chartered Institute of Marketing defines marketing as:

*"the process which identifies, anticipates and satisfies **customers' requirements** profitably"*.

Marketing finds out what products or services customers want or need and provides them at a price which leaves a profit for the business.

Modern marketing management is very **customer focused**; it asks what they really need and if the business is **meeting those needs**. Such **market-driven** businesses will change the product or service to suit the customer.

Marketing begins with analysis of the social, technological, economic, environmental and political factors that will have an impact on **customer demand** for what the organization offers in the marketplace.

We will be looking later at a range of techniques for **primary market research** (original data and internal company information) and **secondary market research** (published statistics) that can help managers to find out what customers want or need and what they are prepared to pay for.

Then managers can make better-informed decisions about the **marketing mix** – the product, pricing, promotion and place – which can all be summarized in the marketing plan for presentation internally and to various stakeholders: investors, banks, and so on.'

B Development of marketing techniques

Marketing was one of the big ideas of the twentieth century. Peter Drucker described it simply as 'creating and keeping customers'. **Customer focus** distinguishes successful organizations from their less successful competitors.

Marketing as a formal management discipline first emerged in post-war America, when the **supply of goods** began to grow more rapidly than **consumer demand** for them. Manufacturers found that in the face of increased competition they had to rethink their attitudes to business. The old ways of operating were no longer working. These included '**production-led**' approaches that assume that if a product is of sufficiently high quality, people will buy it without any further sales effort and '**sales-led**' approaches that put all their energy into selling the goods to customers. Where the **high-pressure sales approach** fails is in establishing long-term business relationships with customers which leads to true success.

In its early days, marketing was used to help sell **tangible products** such as cars, **'white' goods** such as freezers and washing machines for the home and **FMCG** ('fast moving consumer goods') such as groceries and detergent. Later, the basic principles of marketing were adapted to provide a clear structure for making significant management decisions in public sectors such as education and financial services. Even more recently, interesting work is being done to **apply marketing principles** in charitable organizations and the arts.

More recently, companies have found significant benefit in drawing attention to the use of **environmentally friendly materials** in the manufacturing processes used in their product portfolio. Organizations in every sector are making use of high levels of **customer service**, Web 2.0 and social media to complement, or even replace, traditional forms of **promotional material** and advertising.

11.1 Find six word combinations using **customer**. Use texts A and B to help you.

11.2 Complete this student's notes about marketing terms.

apply marketing principles	high-pressure sales approach	market-driven
production-led	sales-led	supply of goods

1 .... = *amount of products produced*
2 .... = *market is dependent on the high standard of the goods*
3 .... = *market is dependent on the number of goods sold*
4 .... = *guided by the needs of the customer*
5 .... = *hard sell*
6 .... = *put theories about marketing into practice*

11.3 Look at the consumer product overview for the Kindle and then answer the questions. Use texts A and B to help you if necessary.

> Amazon – now supplying technical goods to the book-buying public
>
> **The Kindle – Consumer Product Overview**
>
> 1 Revolutionary *electronic-paper* display provides a sharp, high-resolution screen that looks and reads like real paper.
> 2 Simple to use: no computer, no cables, no syncing.
> 3 Wireless connectivity enables you to shop at the Kindle Store directly from your Kindle, whether you're in the back of a taxi, at the airport or in bed.
> 4 Buy a book and it is auto-delivered wirelessly in less than one minute.
> 5 More than 500,000 books, newspapers, magazines and blogs available.
> 6 Lighter and thinner than a typical paperback; weighs only 10.3 ounces.
> 7 Holds over 200 titles.
> 8 Long battery life. Leave wireless on and recharge approximately every other day. Turn wireless off and read for a week or more before recharging. Fully recharges in two hours.
> 9 Unlike Wi-Fi, you never have to locate a hotspot.
> 10 No monthly wireless bills, service plans, or commitments – we take care of the wireless delivery so you can simply click, buy and read.

1 To what extent is the Kindle environmentally friendly?
2 Would you describe the Kindle as a tangible product, a 'white' good or an FMCG?
3 Where would you expect to find promotional materials advertising the Kindle?
4 What other goods might form part of the same product portfolio as the Kindle?
5 According to the product overview, what kind of customer service does the manufacturer of the Kindle provide in order to meet customer needs and wants?
6 Which of your own personal consumer demands does this product respond to?

Over to you

Think of a product or service your organization provides or a consumer product you use. How would you answer the questions in 11.3 to create a consumer product overview?

12 Marketing planning

A   The benefits of marketing planning

Organizations succeed by creating and keeping customers. **Marketing managers** regularly have to assess which customers they are trying to reach and how they can design products and services that provide better value and benefits, delivering **competitive advantage** over competitors in their sector. This process is known as **marketing planning**. A formal **marketing plan** can help managers identify and analyse future opportunities to meet customer needs by defining attractive **market segments** of customers who have certain characteristics in common.

Marketing planning is based on an analysis of the company's customers, competitors and significant factors in the external environment and of its **internal performance**. The contents of a strategic marketing plan are as follows:

- **Mission statement**: setting out the purpose of the organization and covering its role, business definition, distinctive competence and future direction
- **Market overview**: a brief picture of the market, including **market structure, market trends**, key market segments and (sometimes) **gap analysis**
- **SWOT analysis**: analysing the **strengths and weaknesses** of the organization compared with competitors as well as **opportunities and threats** in the external environment
- **Underlying assumptions** critical to the planned **marketing objectives**
- **Marketing objectives**, usually consisting of quantitative statements of the profit, volume and **market share** the organization wishes to achieve
- **Marketing strategies**: stating how the objectives are to be achieved
- **Resource requirements** and the full budget, giving the revenues and associated costs for each year.

B   SWOT analysis – Caffè Italia, a UK coffee retail outlet

The following table appears in a student's marketing assignment:

Strengths	Weaknesses
Caffè Italia is a UK coffee brand **built upon a reputation** for fine products and services.	Some of the company's personnel still lack essential skills.
This **global retailer** is a respected employer that values its workforce.	The company **is over-dependent** on the retailing of coffee, and should consider **diversifying**.
The organization has strong **ethical values** and an ethical mission statement.	

Opportunities	Threats
Opening new locations and branches to **exploit market development** while expanding its range.	Another type of beverage or leisure activity may replace coffee in the future.
Co-branding with other manufacturers of food and drink and **brand franchising** to manufacturers of other goods and services have **potential**.	Caffè Italia **is exposed to** rises in the cost of coffee.
Caffè Italia should consider **extending its market presence** into Asia.	The success of Caffè Italia has led to the **market entry** of many **copy-cat brands** that now pose a potential threat.

12.1 Find eleven word combinations with **market** and **marketing** using words from A and B.

12.2 Read the five definitions and match them to word combinations from 12.1.

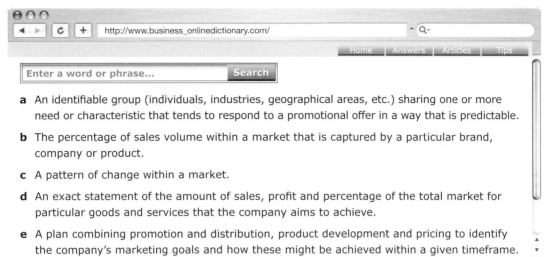

a An identifiable group (individuals, industries, geographical areas, etc.) sharing one or more need or characteristic that tends to respond to a promotional offer in a way that is predictable.

b The percentage of sales volume within a market that is captured by a particular brand, company or product.

c A pattern of change within a market.

d An exact statement of the amount of sales, profit and percentage of the total market for particular goods and services that the company aims to achieve.

e A plan combining promotion and distribution, product development and pricing to identify the company's marketing goals and how these might be achieved within a given timeframe.

12.3 Using words from A and B complete the statements about a competitor to Caffè Italia, Coffee Independent. (You will need to change the form of the nouns in brackets.) Then decide if the statements represent Strengths (S), Weaknesses (W), Opportunities (O) or Threats (T).

 a With its new fair-trade product lines the organization is set to update its mission statement to reflect its .... values.
 b Coffee Independent is a brand built upon a .... for outstanding customer service.
 c Coffee Independent's recent attempts at establishing a market .... in France have not been entirely .... (*profit*).
 d The company has earned respect amongst competitors for its ability to .... (*exploitation*) opportunities for market development and .... (*diversification*) when necessary.
 e Like some of its competitors, as Coffee Independent is a global ...., it is likely to be .... (*exposure*) to political problems in countries where it has operations.
 f In some regions of the UK the company does not have enough branches to ensure market ....
 g Coffee Independent has recently .... (*expansion*) its range of coffees and now includes fair-trade products.
 h The company .... (*dependent*) quite significantly .... a relatively outdated IT system which threatens its ability to .... with the larger global ....
 i The company has been approached as a potential partner in a co-..................... venture to sell products under the same brand name.
 j Despite the arrival of .... brands onto the market recently, Coffee Independent has maintained its lead on the local market.
 k The results of a new gap .... point to potential markets in the Middle East. However, this would involve significant resource .... and a complete review of internal ....

Over to you

Explore www.marketingteacher.co.uk for a fuller description of SWOT analysis from a marketing perspective.

Give at least one example of your organization's internal strengths and weaknesses and any opportunities and threats you can identify in the external environment.

13 The marketing mix

The four Ps / the seven Ps of the marketing mix

The marketing mix refers to the key activities used in marketing an organization's products or services. It is frequently referred to as the **four Ps**:

- **Product** – the features and benefits of the product or service provided
- **Price** – the costs of production, prices charged by the competitors and customers' expectations
- **Promotion** – how to promote and advertise the product or service, i.e. how to communicate with customers
- **Place** – how to **distribute the product** and make it available for consumers, e.g. through **retail outlets** or via the Internet

Some people argue that three other Ps should be added to the marketing mix, especially for organizations that provide **intangible services** that are generally consumed at the time of purchase and may depend on significant human input rather than **tangible products**:

- *People* – those involved in the **delivery of services** to consumers; for example, staff serving in a restaurant are as important as the food on the plate.
- *Process* – how will you deliver the services offered?
- *Physical evidence* – what **premises** (such as factories and offices), or other **tangibles** do you need?

Senior managers can control the elements of the marketing mix to keep ahead of competition. The marketing mix can vary at different times throughout the **product life cycle.**

Product life cycle

Some products have a very long **lifespan**, requiring a series of different marketing mixes. For example, the price may be reduced or advertising might be increased at times when sales are declining. Other items go out of fashion quickly. The product life cycle is the path of a product from the very beginning through to withdrawal from the market, with six separate stages:

- *Research and development (R&D)* – market research is carried out and the product's technical **feasibility** tested, before the product is put on the market.
- *Introduction or launch* – emphasis is placed on **promotion** to build up **product awareness**, encouraging interest in its features and benefits and creating a desire to buy it.
- *Growth* – sales grow rapidly as most customers **are aware of the product**, many have tried it and are starting to develop **customer loyalty**.
- *Maturity* – sales levels are maintained and the product has an established place in the market. Competition may become very intense.
- *Saturation* – supply is plentiful and it is difficult to find new customers.
- *Decline* – sales of the product have fallen. They are not covering the manufacturing costs and the product is therefore unprofitable. The well-prepared business will have a second product ready for introduction to the market to replace the **declining product**.

13.1 Find six word combinations in A and B for the word **product**.

13.2 Choose the correct definition of each of these words or phrases from A and B.

customer loyalty	intangible service	premises	product life cycle	retail outlets

a Something a company provides to customers that cannot be touched or stored.
b A place where goods or services are sold directly to the customer, e.g. a shop or services supplied face to face, e.g. a hairdressing salon.
c A building used for business purposes.
d When people regularly buy the same brand of product because they feel confident that it will meet their needs and wants.
e The identifiable stages from when a product or service is first designed to when it can no longer be sold on the market.

13.3 Use A to label the columns in this table representing the marketing strategy of a chain offering domestic help for the elderly, based on the seven Ps.

1	2	3	4	5	6	7
All employees are well trained; uniforms give a smart, professional appearance.	Employees have a specific client list. A relationship is built and the client feels secure. Supervisors regularly check client satisfaction.	Networking at health sector events, advertising in local newspapers, website.	Researching costs (pay rates, numbers of staff required) that are affordable to government organizations or charities.	Providing a care service for elderly people so they can live with dignity and comfort in their own homes.	Delivery of the service is directly to clients in their own homes.	Establishment of one office per town to ensure recognisable market presence, website aimed at clients, families and healthcare professionals.

13.4 Label the diagram putting the activities (a–e) into a logical sequence (1–5), according to the product life cycle in B.

a Develop and understand corporate goals and strategies to develop replacement products.
b Develop marketing mix.
c Develop strategy, identify and target market segment, differentiate from competitors.
d Implement and control – provide resources to undertake development of replacement product.
e Analyse and understand customer needs and wants, evaluate competition, monitor the environment, conduct market research and consider product lifespan.

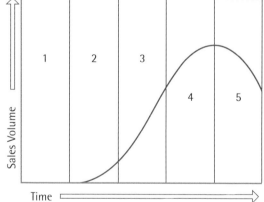

Over to you
Identify at least TWO products or services with which you are familiar that are at the following stages in the product life cycle: Introduction, Early growth, Maturity, Decline.

14 Market research

A STEEP analysis

Martin is a senior manager in a major supermarket chain. He is speaking to an MBA class about how he and his team make significant business decisions:

'As you may know, **STEEP analysis** involves examining the social, technological, economic, environmental and political factors that affect an organization. It generally relates to a **marketing** and **strategic instrument** for **scanning** the macro environment in which we carry out our business activities. Regular use of such a **management instrument** can help us find opportunities for growth and set a clear direction for our operations.

The first slide gives you a clear idea of what the acronym STEEP stands for …'

STEEP Analysis

Social
- Changing demographics over time, based on patterns of birth, death, etc. in the population
- Changes in lifestyle, recreation and leisure patterns
- Changes in social trends, including migration patterns

Technological
- Information technology for business management
- Social networking

Economic
- General economic trends and changes in local, national and global markets
- Tax and insurance

Environmental
- Energy efficiency and **sustainability**, using raw materials and energy in a manner that does not harm the environment
- Reducing our consumption of **raw materials** and energy and recycling our **waste material**
- The **'green' agenda** and the impact of a **carbon footprint**

Political
- EU and national **legislation**, including changes in Health & Safety laws
- **Trade unions** and industry bodies
- Local and national party politics and potential elections.

B Market research methods

Mansour, a partner in a consultancy firm specializing in market research for banks and insurance companies, talking to students conducting a marketing project:

'In each **assignment**, we are trying to **establish the market** for a proposed product or service. We work closely with our client to establish the **research brief**, gathering information about a product's history and **competitive position**, the scale of the project and its likely timescale and costs.

We can sometimes make use of **secondary research data** that has already been compiled about similar products or industry sectors and may be available in business libraries or online.

In the main **data collection stage** we use a range of survey methods, including:

- **questionnaires** that we can deliver face to face, by telephone or online using a resource such as *SurveyMonkey* after **determining a suitable sample** of the total population of **likely customers**
- agendas for discussion in **semi-structured interviews** with **focus groups** and **consumer panels** containing current or potential users of the proposed product or service.

Some research helps us gather **quantitative data**, based on numbers and percentages, and other research is **qualitative**, helping us to understand customers' values, beliefs and behaviour.

The final stage involves the **analysis of the data**, the preparation of the **findings** and recommendations and the creation of the final assignment report for our client.'

14.1 Put the following examples under the correct heading in the STEEP analysis table below:

> a Carbon footprint
> b Consumer trends
> c Implementation of a 'green agenda'
> d Interest rates
> e Legislation in relation to Health & Safety in the workplace
> f Local by-laws
> g Local demographic changes – following the impact of economic migration
> h Recycling of waste products
> i Trade unions
> j Use of online social networking for communicating with other businesses & clients
> k Use of sustainable forestation for purchasing of raw materials

S	T	E	E	P

14.2 Find three terms in A with the word **instrument**. Then find one or more suitable synonyms for the word instrument, as it is used in this context.

14.3 Following the talk by Mansour Said Ali, the students are asked to describe how they carried out their marketing project. Complete Elspeth Goetz's description using terms from B.

'I'm a bit of a health freak and as I knew the producers of the local spring water were trying to .... the market in the region, I proposed my services free of charge. The marketing manager determined a .... sample and my .... brief for the .... was to survey the consumption pattern for the 20–25 age group, the .... of which would then be put to a .... panel for further analysis. The data .... stage was fun but I did spend a lot of time designing the..................... so that it could be used both face to face in .... interviews as well as via an online resource. I know the .... position of this particular producer is currently fairly poor, but I hope that on .... of the data I was able to collect they will see the potential at least for this particular age group of .... customers.'

Over to you

Prepare a STEEP analysis for a product you know well to be marketed in your country or region.

What factors identified in your STEEP analysis have a particular impact on your organization's marketing strategy? (You may wish to look at www.mintel.com or www.keynote.co.uk to help with this.)

15 Using the Internet for marketing

A Market research online

Nick, who runs a specialist consultancy firm based in Zurich, is speaking on a weekly podcast on his firm's website:

'We provide specialist information and advice for clients who need specialist glass packaging for their products.

In the last ten years the Internet has helped us to improve the quality and quantity of the work we do in carrying out market research assignments for our clients. We can **go online** and use sophisticated **search techniques** to gather data and information from industry associations, periodicals and government agencies. We make a lot of use of **online communities** in which we can read and contribute to **blogs** that have been developed by other organizations and individuals. This is a cost-effective (but time-consuming) way of getting our name in front of potential clients and suppliers. *LinkedIn* is a **social networking site** for businesses and for professional people to collaborate with their peers and to extend their networks by taking part in **communities of practice** that are related to their professional interests.

SurveyMonkey allows us to create, distribute and analyse the results from **online questionnaires** more easily than **traditional methods** using postage and reply-paid envelopes.

More recently, we have begun to provide **search engine optimization** to help clients to improve their ranking in search engines and to increase the '**stickiness**' of their website, so that visitors stay on the site for longer.'

B *The Long Tail* and *Freemium*

Professor Kirk is discussing the reading list for an assignment on marketing and the Internet:

'It is well worth looking at two books by Chris Anderson that appear on your reading list. *The Long Tail*, published in 2006, shows how the Internet can provide business opportunities, especially for products and services that can be provided **digitally**, to give more choice and access to **niche markets**, that is small specialist markets, that were previously unprofitable. He gives the example of how the music industry has had to change to use **digital downloads** and **streaming media**.

More recently in *Freemium* he has explored companies that offer **basic online services** or a basic **downloadable** digital product for free and then **charge a premium** for advanced or special features. These can encourage the creation of user-generated content, where individuals can contribute their knowledge and experience to help others. For example, *Google* provides basic services such as email, photo sharing and a suite of programs that allow users to create and collaborate on documents in an **online environment**, and then **charges subscriptions** for **premium services** as well as **content-related advertising**.'

15.1 Complete word combinations for the word **online** using six examples from A and B. The first one is done for you.

go		
	online	

15.2 Use expressions in the box to complete this advertisement for SMM, a provider of social media marketing.

advertisers	blog	communities	digital	downloadable	networking
niche	optimization	podcasts	premium	questionnaires	stickiness
subscription					

http://www.SMMwebads.com/

SMM will design you a .... to enable you to reach clients from your particular .... market as well as access the relevant .... of practice through existing social .... sites. SMM can also help boost awareness of your website, by ensuring search engine .... Give potential customers up-to-the-minute information on your product line. Have existing clients post testimonials and participate in online .... An informal non-sales approach allowing you to interact directly with your customers and gain valuable insight into their needs and wants.

If technology is an issue, then SMM has the know-how. Get potential customers excited about your latest service by sending them .... of interviews with those who have already tried and tested it. Or if it's .... downloads you offer, then send them a .... sample. SMM has the technical means, so sit back and relax.

SMM will also give you that all-important advice on how to exploit the potential of your website: how to attract content-related ....; how to ensure '.....................' so that visitors to your website hang around a little longer; how much to charge for .... services; and how to decide which services to charge a .... for.

Click here

Over to you

Explore Skype and LinkedIn to identify some significant differences between their free products and services and those for which a subscription is required.

Explore www.surveymonkey.com and some related *YouTube* tutorials. Create a simple online survey that you can develop further and use in an organization with which you are familiar.

16 Doing business online

A The four Ps online

Andre, a lecturer in marketing, is talking about effective websites and the impact of the Internet on the marketing mix:

'If a website is to be successful it needs to be relevant to the needs of the **target audience**. We need to ask users what they expect to see and be able to do. Interesting content encourages 'stickiness'; visitors return regularly and spend longer on the site. **Community features** include simple opinion polls, online surveys and **discussion forums** to engage customers and develop a feeling of 'belonging' to the website.

Companies are using the Internet to make decisions about their marketing mix. Products can be **customized** to suit the needs and interests of regular customers. Supermarkets can create **personalized lists** of recommendations based on a shopper's regular purchases. Retailers can ensure that **price comparison websites** feature their products at competitive prices. Company websites can include **interactive features** such as surveys and competitions to build relationships with customers. Software, music and hotel reservations can be **delivered digitally**.'

B Viral marketing in action

Viral marketing (or 'word of mouse marketing') is a method of advertising and promoting a company's products or services in which individuals send information to their friends using a range of online media such as email, blogs, Facebook and other social networking sites.

Buzz marketing operates in a similar way. **Product champions** and **trendsetters** can be identified and encouraged to push products or services. Fashion accessories and smart phones have recently benefited from buzz marketing.

Some companies are moving away from **traditional advertising media** and are starting to make use of short videos as entertainment appealing to a broader range of consumers. One successful example of viral marketing is Cadbury, who used a familiar piece of popular music in their 'Gorilla' advertisement for their chocolate products.

C Doing business online

Dr Dorndorf is introducing an assignment that students are required to complete for her module:

'The challenge in the assignment is to draw clear differences between traditional business processes and the processes used in carrying out **online business**, both **B2C** (a business that deals directly with consumers) and **B2B** (providing goods and services for other businesses).

You can choose to explore the activities of **online retailers** where the business may be **fully online**, such as Amazon, or a **clicks and mortar site**, such as an established retailer that has both **physical outlets** on the High Street and an **online presence**.

Some businesses, such as low-cost airlines, have been able to pass on massive savings in **transaction costs** to their customers.

You may also need to consider consumer concerns about how personal information is collected, **data security** and **online payments** such as PayPal.'

16.1 Match words from the two lists to make collocations related to online retailing.

buzz	online (x2)	advertising media	marketing (x2)
clicks and mortar	physical	audience	online
community	product	business	outlet
discussion	target	champions	retailer
fully	traditional	feature (x2)	site
interactive	viral	forum	

16.2 Use the two-word collocations in 16.1 to complete this article.

Shahara Khan, *Marketing Manager, takes us through a period of transition for SOX.com.*

Voted the fashion industry's .... of the year in 2009, SOX.com started out life as a ....: a small stall in the trendy Spitalfields Market in London. Taking it slowly, SOX.com then became a so-called ...., eventually going .... in 2005. Unlike other .... in the fashion world, it has witnessed phenomenal success, and now stocks over 32,000 styles, with a product range aimed primarily at the 16 to 34 age group, but which in reality appeals to a much wider public. Our use of technology goes beyond ....; one of our more .... is our online 'catwalk', a unique tool enabling *fashionistas* to see our products on moving models. Ours is a relatively young ...., so it's very easy to promote sales through .... – via Facebook, for example. SOX.com also engages in .... to help sell our new lines. We encourage our .... to participate in .... – where they discuss the latest styles available in our online store. Indeed, this .... was only added fairly recently but has proved highly successful ...

16.3 Following her article, Shahara Khan received various questions posted on the discussion forum. Match the two halves to form questions.

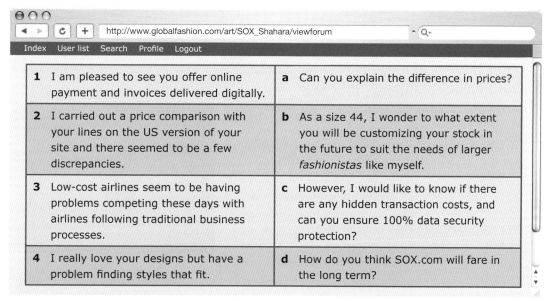

http://www.globalfashion.com/art/SOX_Shahara/viewforum

Index   User list   Search   Profile   Logout

1 I am pleased to see you offer online payment and invoices delivered digitally.	**a** Can you explain the difference in prices?
2 I carried out a price comparison with your lines on the US version of your site and there seemed to be a few discrepancies.	**b** As a size 44, I wonder to what extent you will be customizing your stock in the future to suit the needs of larger *fashionistas* like myself.
3 Low-cost airlines seem to be having problems competing these days with airlines following traditional business processes.	**c** However, I would like to know if there are any hidden transaction costs, and can you ensure 100% data security protection?
4 I really love your designs but have a problem finding styles that fit.	**d** How do you think SOX.com will fare in the long term?

Over to you

Consider your own experience of online retailing. What are the benefits of online retailing? Are there any challenges or problems?

17 Processes

A Managing operations overview

Operations management deals with all aspects of how an organization produces and delivers its products and services. These include its business processes and procedures, its **supply chain** and issues in **quality management.**

The **value chain** is Michael Porter's instrument for considering all the functions that transform inputs into outputs, plus the internal business functions that support the transformation process.

Outsourcing can be another important element in an organization's operations management: should some business processes be kept **in-house** or **subcontracted** to an external supplier?

B Porter's value chain

This model indicates how each of the elements Porter identifies can make significant contributions to the value provided for customers. Improvements in one area can lead to overall improvements in the organization's competitive advantage. Porter identifies two types of activities:

Primary activities

- o *Inbound logistics:* receiving goods into store, stock control
- o *Operations:* production processes, packaging, testing of **finished goods**
- o *Outbound logistics:* how the company gets its finished goods to the customers, transportation
- o *Marketing and sales:* promotion, pricing, selling
- o *Service:* installation, customer training, customer support.

Support activities

- o *Procurement:* obtaining raw materials, equipment and machinery, maintenance of equipment
- o *Technology development:* R&D (research and development), design
- o *Human resource management:* recruitment, development, reward of staff
- o *Organizational infrastructure:* planning, finance, legal, management.

C Contingency planning and risk

Margaret is a lecturer introducing a new module on an MBA programme:

'Today's businesses are exposed to ever-changing **global risks,** from volcanic ash to major financial challenges.

Senior managers must be able **to assess risk** accurately and to understand where their business may be **vulnerable.** They need to be able to put in place a **risk management process** to **deal with risk** and an effective **contingency plan** if necessary.

Successful organizations will be **risk aware,** and will have confidence in their ability to **identify** and **avoid potential risks** that come from both predictable and unpredictable changes in the environment in which they operate. We will look at how companies produce **risk profiles** and develop systems to **prioritize risks** which eventually form their **risk management policies.**

Visiting speakers on this module will include senior staff involved in **risk and continuity management** as well as **emergency planning** officers and **business continuity** managers.'

17.1 Match the descriptions to the explanations of Porter's value chain to complete the PowerPoint slides.

1	Inbound logistics	**a**	The storage and distribution of the finished goods
2	Outbound logistics	**b**	The purchasing of all goods, raw materials and services needed to create the product or service
3	Service	**c**	The receiving and storing of raw materials from suppliers, and then distributing them to where they are needed
4	Procurement	**d**	The activities that help improve the efficiency or effectiveness of the primary activities
5	Organizational infrastructure	**e**	The organization and control of finance, legal matters and information technology
6	Support activities	**f**	The activities that are directly concerned with making the product or delivering the service
7	Primary activities	**g**	The support for customers after they have bought the product, including installing the product, delivering after-sales service and handling complaints

17.2 Find ten word combinations using the word **risk** from C and place them in the correct column.

Noun phrase	Verb phrase	Adjectival phrase
	prioritize risks	

17.3 Alain is senior manager in an oil exploration company. Read his explanation of the steps his company took to develop a risk-management process. Complete his strategy using A, B and C to help you. Then put the strategy steps into the correct order.

1 From this analysis, we have established an effective risk .... across the organization by:
  ■ systematically identifying, evaluating and prioritizing .... risks. For this we have a written risk .... that sets out responsibilities of key staff.
  ■ developing an organizational culture in which individuals are risk .... but are not afraid of taking decisions and undertaking activities which involve acceptable levels of risk.

2 We regularly collect data and evaluate information to monitor further risks and review the .... plans which have been put in place. We also monitor and review the effectiveness of the risk .... in the company, identifying potential improvements and making changes where necessary.

3 As part of the .... team, I chair a working group to evaluate and monitor both our current and our planned projects to identify the nature of the risks, the probability of occurrence and the consequences. From this we produce a .... so that we can see where the company might be .... and then .... the identified risks.

4 We identify .... risks as well as issues that could affect us on a more local scale, such as the risk to our .... chain, as we rely a lot on .... and we also .... processes to external suppliers.

5 We then pass all this information on to our .... officers and .... managers, who ensure continuity of service to our key customers and the protection of our reputation following a disruptive event.

Over to you

Visit the Institute of Risk Management website at www.theirm.org to find out how the International Standards can help business managers to approach risk management.

18 Suppliers

A Supply chains

Central to the way that companies produce things is the way that they manage their **supply chains** – the collection and distribution of all the inputs to the production process. Much of the improvement in **supply chain management** in recent years has come about through improved information systems that enable managers to know more accurately exactly what is where and when. In many cases improving the efficiency of supply chains also involves changing a company's relationships with its suppliers. Not all suppliers or **subcontractors** are prepared to **bear the extra cost** involved in **holding stock** on their customers' behalf. Those that are want a greater commitment from those customers, which has led companies to become much closer to their suppliers, sometimes establishing a **formal alliance** with them and sometimes taking an **equity stake** in their business. Such a relationship also means having a tighter control over suppliers. This can be done via a **supplier audit** so that **remedial steps can be taken** to ensure tighter control over production.

B Purchasing

Extract from a lecture by Leonardo, who has recently completed a major survey of purchasing procedures in successful organizations:

'So what are the elements in the **purchasing process**? Well, once the need for the product is firmly established, the **procurement department** must **draw up specifications**, to make sure the supplier knows exactly what is required for goods to be **fit for purpose**. Then they have to identify suppliers who can provide the specified products on time and within budget.

The procurement department will often have a list of **approved suppliers** the organization has done business with in the past. In some cases they may use **trade directories**, online databases and other means to research potential suppliers. They also need to carry out a **value analysis** of each item procured to make sure that there is not a more cost-effective substitute.

After the **initial order** is fulfilled the relationship with the new supplier must be managed, especially if the organization is likely to make substantial **repeat purchases** over a considerable period of time.'

C Outsourcing

Senior managers have a responsibility to identify business processes which are not part of their organization's **core competences**. These include not only **payroll management**, cleaning or security but also more complex processes such as helpline provision or product assembly. These can also include **outsourced processes** delivered on the organization's own premises (for example, catering) and processes carried out at the suppliers' premises.

Members of the senior management team need to be able to:

- identify **core** and **non-core business processes** and assess the potential benefits, costs, risks and any legal and ethical implications of outsourcing these processes.

- create a clear specification of requirements.

- shortlist potential **vendors** using a **rating system** and then select the one which best meets the criteria.

- negotiate and agree a **legally binding contract** that specifies the volume and level of service to be provided, payment terms and how performance will be monitored.

- **monitor performance** in line with the contract and review the outsourcing arrangement at agreed points.

18.1 Complete the interview with Charlotte of Hanna.com, Europe's market leader in online fashion retailing by <u>underlining</u> the correct word/expression in each case. Use A to help you.

Q: Hanna.com was named European Online Retailer of the Year in 2011 and I understand your website is currently attracting over five million visitors a month. With so much interest, how do you deal with *supply chain management / supplier audits*?

A: Our *equity stake / supply chain* is run on a fairly traditional basis. In fact we *audit / hold stock* of over 20,000 product styles in our warehouse. We don't expect the supplier to *bear the extra cost / take remedial steps* of storing the products for us.

Q: I understand that some of your *subcontractors / supply chain managers* were accused a few years ago of unethical conduct?

A: Unfortunately, yes. We carried out *formal alliances / supplier audits* in several countries and these careful checks revealed that some *suppliers / formal alliances* had been hiring underage employees. We immediately took *equity stakes / remedial steps* and we've increased the number of factories *audited / holding stock* each year from 29 to 106.

Q: Have you considered creating a *formal alliance / supplier audit* with some of your suppliers so that you work together with their management to avoid similar occurrences?

A: We feel that owning shares in our suppliers is a more effective way to exert control, rather than entering a formal partnership. So having *a formal alliance with / an equity stake in* our subcontractors' companies may well be the way forward.

18.2 Match the words in the lists to find six word combinations from B. Then use four of them to complete the definitions below.

approved   initial   procurement   repeat   trade   value
department   directory   analysis   purchases   suppliers   order

1 The .... is responsible for sourcing and purchasing goods and services needed for the organization's processes and operations.
2 .... involves investigating the cost, quality and likely useful life of an item, to make sure it will give the organization the best value for money after purchase.
3 A/an .... is an extensive published list of companies who supply different types of products and services to other organizations.
4 .... are companies who have fulfilled certain conditions so that they are allowed to offer goods and services to an organization on a regular basis.

18.3 Complete the newspaper article using words or phrases from the box.

core competences	legally binding	monitored	non-core processes
outsourced processes	outsourcing	payroll	rating system	vendors

Cuts May Create Outsourcing Boom

As the public sector faces efficiency drives and budget cuts resulting from the credit crunch, Sue Rippin, business development manager at Northgate Arinso, an HR .... company, expects to see a growth in business. She highlighted councils as prime areas for growth in ...., because their .... remain relatively limited. They are specialists in supplying services such as Health and Education, rather than .... such as .... management. Rippin added that 'outsourcing is very competitive. As ...., offering our services, we are selected using a rigorous .... and have agreed to a .... contract. The standard of our performance will be .... to ensure that we keep to the agreed contract; otherwise we could face legal action'.

Over to you

Think about the goods or services needed by an organization you are familiar with. Which ones are outsourced? What might be the problems of maintaining an appropriate flow of supplies, in terms of cost and timing?

19 Managing quality

A Quality

Management commitment to satisfying the customer involves the creation of a **'quality' culture** and recognition that **'the customer rules'**. It ensures that products and services conform to the customer's requirements and are **fit for purpose**. Meeting a **customer's specification** leads to a satisfied customer, who will provide repeat orders and resist offers from competitors.

The quality of the final product depends upon the quality of the exchanges along the **internal supply chain**, with continuous improvement of internal and external products and services and employees trained to take responsibility for their own outputs. **Quality assurance** is now the subject of international standards and initiatives by bodies such as the International Organization for Standardization (ISO), fostering worldwide development of good practice and providing **benchmarks** so that organizations can compare their standards with the best performers.

B ISO 9001:2008

ISO 9001:2008 is the international standard providing a set of requirements for a **quality management system**, regardless of what the organization does, its size, or whether it is in the private or public sector.

ISO 9001:2008 requires the organization to have **documented procedures** for the approval and control of **critical documents** (for example, production plans, **activity flow-charts**), **critical records** (for example, orders from customers, invoices for goods and services provided) and **internal audit** of the quality management system to verify that it **complies fully with** the standard and manages the organization's processes effectively. Although it lays down what requirements a quality system must meet, it leaves great flexibility for how these are **implemented** in different sectors and business cultures.

C EFQM

The EFQM (European Foundation for Quality Management) Excellence Model provides a basis for achieving **sustainable excellence** for any organization.

Excellent organizations succeed by:

- progressing towards their vision through planning and achieving balanced results, which take into account measures of customer satisfaction, employee satisfaction and business results.
- **adding value** for customers, striving to innovate and create value for them by understanding and anticipating their needs and expectations.
- leading with vision, inspiration and integrity, through leaders who shape the future and make it happen, acting as **role models** for its values and ethics.
- managing through structured and strategically aligned processes using **fact-based decision making**, such as **statistical process control** to create sustained results.
- valuing their people and creating a culture of **empowerment** for the balanced achievement of organizational and personal goals.
- **nurturing creativity** and innovation, generating increased value and levels of performance through continual and systematic innovation by harnessing the creativity of their stakeholders.
- **building partnerships** – seeking, developing and maintaining trusting relationships with various partners, customers, key suppliers or the community to ensure mutual success.
- **embedding** within their culture high standards of organizational behaviour, to strive for economic, social and ecological **sustainability**.

19.1 Find terms in A that correspond to these definitions.

Enter a word or phrase. . .

1 .... – standards used for for evaluating performance or level of quality.

2 .... – a detailed description of what is required.

3 .... – suitable for intended use.

4 .... – the stages through which a product or service moves before it is delivered to the external customer.

5 .... – a system for monitoring and checking that processes, goods and services meet the specified requirements.

6 .... – a phrase meaning that the company policy places the needs and wants of the customer before its own interests or convenience.

19.2 Complete this interview with a representative of the ISO with terms from B.

Q: The effective management of water resources and access to clean drinking water are major concerns for governments. What is the role of the ISO in this process?

A: It is important to understand that our role is not prescriptive; the organization merely provides the guidelines for a ....

Q: What does standardizing service provision worldwide involve?

A: The aim of the ISO is to work with regional and national authorities to determine the level of results to be achieved and then to establish the means by which their procedures are .... As with the private sector, these authorities will be required to .... and demonstrate that they are .... the ISO guidelines. Just as in the case of the private sector, they may carry out a/an ...., that is, an objective internal appraisal of the organization's procedures and performance to ensure compliance.

19.3 Use expressions from C to complete comments from this EFQM judge about the Award Winner 2010.

The Eskisehir Maternity and Child Illness Hospital seeks to provide patients with a level of care that exceeds expectations, with nurses in particular being encouraged to .... directly with their patients, adding value to their experiences through new ways of providing care. By promoting the free circulation of ideas and personal growth the Eskisehir also strives to .... its staff. Indeed this is a hospital that has developed an environment of trust and responsibility, actively .... creativity and innovation from its employees. This means there is a positive mindset .... within the professional environment, which helps to retain its staff and ensure a .... future for the hospital. As well as focusing on the human factor, the hospital employs a sound basis of .... decision making. The organization has achieved a ...., in terms of patient and staff satisfaction as well as economic efficiency. In fact, its performance has demonstrated an ability to act as a .... hospital within the region. The panel felt the Eskisehir had achieved a certain level of .... that merited this year's award.

Over to you

Think about managing quality in an organization you know. What are the main issues? Compare your ideas with the information about quality management standards on the ISO website at www.iso.org

20 Customer care

A Customer relationship management (CRM)

21st-century companies know they have to maintain high standards of quality. Competition is fierce; consumers demand that organizations meet their expectations for excellence.

Professor Jaroslav Vrba introduces the concept of CRM to a group of MBA students:

'As customers become more discriminating, better informed and less **loyal to brands**, organizations have had to identify methods of managing relationships with existing customers and providing better levels of service.

Customer relationship management makes extensive use of information technology and the Internet. Banking and insurance were early movers in this field. They were aware that it costs much more to **recruit a** new **customer** than it does to **retain an existing customer**. Customer loyalty cards provide opportunities for **data mining; data warehousing** can be used to acquire and store information about customers and their **purchasing habits**, so that better-informed decisions can be made about products and services that may appeal to individual **market segments** within the total **customer base**.

The data in the system can also be used to identify opportunities for **cross-selling**. For example, knowledge of significant changes in a customer's life can be used to offer them mortgages or pension plans for retirement.'

B Customer journey mapping

Helena is a local government official, speaking at a conference on improving public services for local communities:

'**Customer journey mapping** helps to identify **contact points** in users' experiences when they use a service from regional or central government. It takes into account not only what happens to them but also their reactions and responses to their experiences. It provides a clear view of government services from the **customer's perspective**. Used well, this technique can reveal opportunities for improvement and innovation. If hotels can do it, why can't we?

Why is this important?

- We recognise that we have to do more **to get closer to customers**, understanding what really drives behaviour and attitudes. Journey mapping, with its focus on **tracking** and describing customer experience, is one of the tools that can help do this.
- Journey mapping helps bring **customers' stories** and experiences to life. It can challenge assumptions and help change perceptions, contributing to **culture change** in the organization.

The insights that it generates can help **shape policy**, leading to better customer experiences and more efficient service delivery by **customer-facing** teams who have direct contact with the customers.'

20.1 Match the questions (1–5) and answers (a–e) following Professor Vrba's session on CRM in A.

'Excuse me, Professor Vrba …

1 … could you clarify the meaning of cross-selling?

2 … you mentioned data warehousing, but I didn't quite understand what you meant.

3 … could you explain the difference between *customer base* and *market segment*?

4 … I was just wondering about data mining. Could you clarify the meaning for us, please?

5 … you talked about purchasing habits, what's the significance of this expression?

a The first refers to the people or organizations who buy or use a particular product. The second refers to a group of consumers who share certain characteristics or lifestyles. These groups tend to respond predictably to a particular marketing offer, for example.

b It's when companies offer customers further products based on information about their purchasing history.

c It's about sorting through databases containing large amounts of information about customers, to reveal trends and patterns that can be useful to the company.

d Tom Hindle suggested it was about '*integrating information about customers and putting it into one huge database*', so the information is stored electronically and can be used in different ways.

e Well, it's crucial in customer relationship management. It basically tells us about customer behaviour, for example, what they buy, how often and where.

20.2 Find expressions from A to match the definitions.

.... – when an individual always buys the product of a particular company rather than similar products offered by other companies

.... – persuading customers to start buying your company's products

.... – making sure that customers continue to purchase your product or service

.... – systematic policies to monitor and ensure customer satisfaction

20.3 A spokesperson for Eurostar explains the outcomes of customer journey mapping. Complete the article using expressions from B.

The appointment of our new Chief Executive with a marketing background acted as an important catalyst in bringing about c.................... change and s.................... p.................... to make Eurostar more customer orientated.

He suggested we bring our c.................... s.................... to life by using c.................... j.................... m.................... . This was carried out using a heart monitor, t.................... the highs and lows of the journey – the c.................... p.................... where they interacted with c....................-f.................... staff or machines, the times when people became bored or even experienced fear, for example, when entering the tunnel. By making the journey themselves, staff were able to get c.................... to their c....................s.

After experiencing the service from the c....................'s p...................., staff suggested really practical solutions to problems, which not only improved the experience but, in many cases, reduced costs too.

Over to you

Think about the customer journey in interacting with your organization. What are the customer contact points? How could you track their experience? Who would collect information and how?

21 Operations online

A Just-in-time and online inventory management

Bror is speaking at his retirement party in the purchasing department of a major Scandinavian engineering company:

'When I joined the company we used a traditional **stock control system**. We kept large stocks of material to give us a **margin of safety** in the warehouse to cope with sudden orders, or with poor quality, or to get the benefits of **discounts** for quantities using **economies of scale**. We set our **reorder levels** to ensure that we had some **buffer stock**, but this meant that a huge amount of the company's money was tied up in **inventory**, raw materials or components sitting on the shelves waiting to be used.

Later, in the 1980s, we moved to the Japanese **just-in-time** approach (JIT) where a signal automatically triggers an order in the company's purchasing system when an item is used. Now, of course, this is underpinned by a **state-of-the-art** web-based **inventory management system** which tracks our stock levels and the current status of any purchase orders we have made, so there is no costly storage or unused stock.'

B Online tendering

Cameroon – Invitation to Tender for Construction at University of Buea

Open International Invitation to Tender for the Construction of a Teaching Laboratory Block and Landscaping for the Faculty of Health Sciences at the University of Buea, Cameroon.

Nature of Service:
The construction of a Teaching Laboratory Block (R+2) of study laboratories, research laboratories and offices (LOT 1), on the one hand and Landscaping comprising the construction of parking area, pavements, lighting, roads, gutters, planting of grass and trees on the other hand (LOT 2).
Please note that the administrative file of each bidder must contain a bid bond as follows:
Lot 1: 26,000,000 F CFA (approx £32,500)
Lot 2: 19,000,000 F CFA (approx £23,750)

Fiona runs a small company that provides an online service for businesses in the construction and related sectors throughout Scotland:

'Each week private and public organizations **put out to tender** work they require for their building projects. This means formal advertisements are published in newspapers or on the Internet, inviting suppliers to make an offer to provide these services. We put all these on our website, together with a set of **tender documents** with full details of the requirements and **specifications** for each project. By paying a **subscription** to our online service, our clients get access to a larger number of potential business opportunities where they may be **prospective suppliers**. They can download the tender documents and **put in a tender**, that is, submit an offer to provide the services.

We endeavour to make this site as **'user-friendly'** as possible, with clear **guidance notes** about procedures for resolving any **pre-tender queries** and information about how the **tenders will be evaluated**, and we carefully research the answers to our **FAQs** (frequently asked questions) pages. Registered users can even take part in our discussion forums, to compare experiences.

Of course, many large organizations use their own **online procurement system** that allows **tenderers** to download the documents and submit a bid electronically via the Internet. These **secure online systems** even store and **encrypt** submissions to **ensure confidentiality**.

These days more and more organizations who wish to **source** products or services are able to make use of their own **online systems** or commercial services like ours to identify potential suppliers and compare the products and support services they offer, to make most efficient use of their **procurement budgets**.'

21.1 Majed is introducing the topic of online inventory management to students on an MBA course. Find words or phrases from A that have the same meaning as the underlined phrases.

A few years ago companies used to think in terms of just <u>controlling and monitoring the supplies or goods stored in the company</u> (1).

These days manufacturers take a more active approach to <u>managing the flow of supplies and materials needed for their processes</u> (2). This relies on the <u>most technically advanced</u> (3) software systems for tracking purchases and <u>monitoring the actual stock on the shelves</u> (4). They also reorder new stock when the existing stock reaches <u>a certain minimum quantity</u> (5).

When holding stock, there needs to be <u>enough spare capacity for emergencies</u> (6), so companies usually kept <u>spare items</u> (7) for this purpose. However, a more modern approach is to have a very quick turnaround, so that supplies are ordered and arrive <u>just at the time when they are needed</u> (8). Of course, the disadvantage of this system is that manufacturers lose the <u>price reductions</u> (9) they might have obtained by achieving <u>reduced costs by producing or buying large amounts of something</u> (10).

21.2 Look at B and find five expressions using the word **tender.** Also find a noun for suppliers who offer their goods and services. Now try to write your own definition of the **noun** tender in its business meaning. Check your answer with the dictionary definition given in the answers.

21.3 Complete the article from the business section of a newspaper, using words from B.

Richard Maybey, a manager in a major European financial services group, was asked about his experience of using online p.................... services.

'I am responsible for an annual procurement b.................. of 20m euros. Major areas in which I have to s.................. goods and services include IT equipment and catering and cleaning services.

In recent years we have moved to a robust system to p....................our requirements o....................to t..................... I simply upload the t.................... d.................... with our particular s.................... to our website and wait for the suppliers to contact me and the time taken to find p.................... s.................... is significantly reduced. The process is a s.................... online system and even uses a code to e.................... the private details the suppliers provide about their business to ensure confidentiality.

We have also used commercial online tendering services. The only problem I find with services targeting the financial sector is that the sites are not always u.................... and lack g.................... notes to take you through the features of the site. And if you have any p.................... q...................., the information in the F.................... page is often insufficient. However, there is sometimes a d.................... f...................., where you can actually talk about issues with other people in the same line of work. There is often a section where people c.................... their experiences, good or bad, of particular suppliers, which can be useful, but this is only for r.................... u.................... so you need a s.................... first. The cost of this payment can be quite high.'

Over to you

Use the terms "online inventory management benefits" in a search engine to find out how this technique can help a business with which you are familiar.

22 Recruitment and selection

A The recruitment and selection process

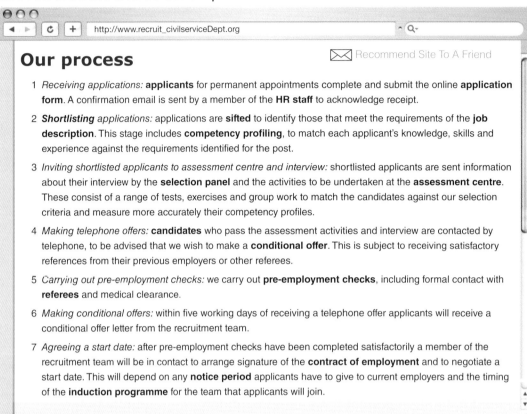

Our process   ✉ Recommend Site To A Friend

1 *Receiving applications:* **applicants** for permanent appointments complete and submit the online **application form**. A confirmation email is sent by a member of the **HR staff** to acknowledge receipt.

2 *Shortlisting applications:* applications are **sifted** to identify those that meet the requirements of the **job description**. This stage includes **competency profiling**, to match each applicant's knowledge, skills and experience against the requirements identified for the post.

3 *Inviting shortlisted applicants to assessment centre and interview:* shortlisted applicants are sent information about their interview by the **selection panel** and the activities to be undertaken at the **assessment centre**. These consist of a range of tests, exercises and group work to match the candidates against our selection criteria and measure more accurately their competency profiles.

4 *Making telephone offers:* **candidates** who pass the assessment activities and interview are contacted by telephone, to be advised that we wish to make a **conditional offer**. This is subject to receiving satisfactory references from their previous employers or other referees.

5 *Carrying out pre-employment checks:* we carry out **pre-employment checks**, including formal contact with **referees** and medical clearance.

6 *Making conditional offers:* within five working days of receiving a telephone offer applicants will receive a conditional offer letter from the recruitment team.

7 *Agreeing a start date:* after pre-employment checks have been completed satisfactorily a member of the recruitment team will be in contact to arrange signature of the **contract of employment** and to negotiate a start date. This will depend on any **notice period** applicants have to give to current employers and the timing of the **induction programme** for the team that applicants will join.

B Recruitment of temporary staff

Roberto is responsible for the recruitment of temporary staff to work in his events management company on projects across Europe.

'Because our business model is quite simple, we do not need a sophisticated **human resources strategy**. We do sixty per cent of our business in the summer months, providing services at golf tournaments and music concerts, for example. We need approximately 1,000 staff on **temporary contracts** in June, July and August to service this level of business, most of whom are **hired** through **online recruitment services** and social media such as Facebook. We seldom place **job advertisements** in newspapers. Some of these temporary workers are later appointed to **permanent posts** in our organization.'

C Employment legislation and equal opportunities

An organization committed to **equality** welcomes **diversity** amongst its **workforce** and seeks to **comply** fully **with current legislation**. Many employers make public statements to the effect that **discrimination** will not occur in relation to age, ethnicity, sexual orientation or religious beliefs. Part-time workers must receive **equal treatment** to full-time staff. Employers have to assist people with disabilities to gain **equal access** to all the employment benefits that are available to other staff. While complaints most commonly arise at the recruitment stage, employers should ensure that **equal opportunities** are embedded in all their **employment policies**.

22.1 Complete the explanation for each of the points Roberto mentions in his procedure for recruitment. Use A and B to help you. Then put the steps into the most appropriate order.

- Screening the applicants: completed application .... are .... to ensure that we only interview suitable candidates. Apart from interviews, we also use .... centres where we carry out .... profiling.

- Person requirements: we draw up a job .... profiling ...., that is the skills and the knowledge required to do the job as well as the essential attitudes or characteristics to fit into the organization.

- Job ....: this is usually done online.

- .... programme: every new member of the team spends a day with the team with whom they will be working. They are introduced to the working procedure and different team roles.

- Invitation to interview: we then ask the .... selected from the screening process (the .... candidates) to attend a selection .... in which a group of interviewers explore the skills, qualifications and knowledge they can bring to the job.

- Resources requirement: our .... strategy, that is, identifying why we are recruiting and how to match the people we employ and the jobs they do to our company's goals, is an important element of our annual planning.

- Appointment: after the interviews have been completed we make a .... offer and contact the .... once the successful candidate has accepted the terms and conditions of their .... of .... They then have to work out their .... period, that is the length of time they have to continue working for their present employer after they officially resign from that job.

22.2 Find four new words or expressions from C using the base word **equal**.

22.3 Correct the mistakes in this extract from this company website. Some of the underlined words or expressions are in the wrong place. Use C to help you.

QualityTime plc has a robust <u>current</u> <u>legislation</u> policy. That means we welcome applications from all sections of the community, regardless of race, religion, disability or other differences. In fact, we believe that this <u>workforce</u> in our <u>diversity</u> is a strength of our organization.

We also believe that <u>equal treatment</u> against any group of workers has no place in a modern company. We comply with <u>equal access</u> under UK and EU law, and under our <u>employment</u> policies, <u>discrimination</u> is guaranteed for all members of staff, including those on <u>current legislation</u> contracts or part-time workers as well as full-time employees.

Over to you

Use the term "recruitment and selection process" in a search engine to find out more about policies and procedures used in several different types of organization.

23 | Motivation and job design

A | Herzberg

In his seminal article on employee **motivation** Frederick Herzberg distinguishes between events or changes likely to lead to an increase in **job satisfaction** ('motivators') and events or changes likely to cause job dissatisfaction if missing, but not affect the person's job satisfaction ('**hygiene factors**', such as pay, status and working conditions). Good hygiene in a restaurant does not increase the customers' enjoyment but poor hygiene affects their health or satisfaction. In a similar way, the well-being and job satisfaction of employees depends on these problems being avoided.

In general, the stronger the person's feeling about any one of the 'motivators', the stronger the person's satisfaction and sense of engagement.

Factors that lead to satisfaction	*Factors that lead to dissatisfaction*
• A **sense of achievement** when challenging targets are reached • The **recognition of achievement** by their **peers, and a collaborative environment**, with opportunities to receive praise and reward • The work itself • Responsibility and opportunities to **take charge of** significant projects • Opportunities for **advancement** and **career development** in an organization where they feel they have **job security**.	• *Company policy*, '**red tape**' and administration • Too much supervision and a feeling of being **micro managed** • Low **salary levels** • Strained or hostile **interpersonal relationships** with **colleagues** at work • Uncomfortable **working conditions**.

B | Hackman and Oldham's job characteristics model

Performance and commitment in the workplace improve if individuals are given **autonomy** and responsibility for clearly defined tasks (including being able to complete an activity or job in full), can use **a wide variety of skills**, can make decisions and solve problems, and get meaningful **feedback** on results and about their performance. According to Hackman procedures that can lead to improvements in performance and commitment in the workplace are:

- **Job rotation** – moving people regularly between different sets of tasks.

- **Job enlargement** – giving an individual a larger number of broadly similar tasks.

- **Job enrichment** – adding extra tasks that involve more decision-making, and increased autonomy.

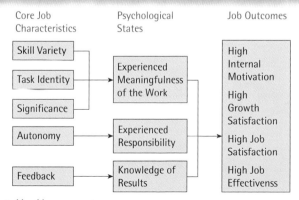

23.1 Find definitions from A and B using the word **job** to match these remarks from HR managers.

1 'Some were reluctant to leave their initial placements, but eventually they appreciated the value of moving round and realised it provided them with additional new skills.'

2 'Staff often find this sort of 'horizontal' as opposed to vertical expansion of their role within the division very rewarding.'

3 'The likelihood these days of my staff being able to remain in the same job for the rest of their life is highly improbable.'

4 'The results of the survey showed that having a sense of control, a feeling of accomplishment, and a complex job contributed to their positive attitude toward the job.'

5 'Whereas previously they'd reported to a supervisor, we gave them lots more control so that they felt they actually planned and carried out the job.'

23.2 Match Hackman and Oldham's job characteristics to phrases a–e.

1	Autonomy	a	Receiving an evaluation of your performance
2	Feedback	b	For example, constructing signs for the Olympic Games will be more satisfying for a sports fan than making signs for a new shopping mall
3	Skill variety	c	Being allowed to solve problems and perform a wider range of non-routine tasks
4	Task identity	d	Being involved in decisions, instead of being told what to do
5	Significance	e	For example, sewing an entire dress would be more satisfying to a worker than just sewing buttons onto it

23.3 Complete Stella's comments about her job at a UN agency using words from the box.

advancement	charge	collaborative	colleagues	conditions
engagement	interpersonal	micro	motivation	peers
personal	recognition	red	reputation	salary
satisfaction	well-being			

'Working for the UN, I feel a certain sense of ...., with the work itself, because it is contributing to the greater good. Also I have good .... relationships with my .... who work beside me in the team because it is a really .... work environment. However, international organizations have a reputation for top-heavy administrative procedures and .... tape, you know, too many unimportant rules often resulting in too much .... management.

Sadly for secretaries there is little in terms of career .... and .... development and .... levels are low. Most of my ...., that is, the other secretaries who work at the same level as me, are multilingual, and we frequently act as unofficial interpreters, as well as taking .... of extremely sensitive UN documents. However, while working .... are generally good and the employee's .... is taken into consideration, ... remains low. There is little .... of our achievements, a critical factor in terms of overall job ....'

Over to you

Use the terms "motivation reward how to" in a search engine to find out more about policies and procedures used in several different types of organization.

24 Performance appraisal, feedback, training and development

A 360-degree feedback

Significant changes in organizational structures in recent years, with **flattened hierarchies**, **virtual teams** and greater **employee empowerment**, have implications for the appraisal process. An individual's colleagues may be in a better position to judge his or her performance than before.

360-degree feedback collects information from all around an individual employee and may be used in an organization as an alternative to a traditional **performance appraisal** system. It involves **self-assessment** by an individual and an appraisal (normally using some form of **online appraisal system**) by those above, below and to the side of the individual employee. Such feedback is anonymous; it is provided through an independent and objective **facilitator**, so that opinions given and statements made cannot be traced to individuals. The process includes:

- *peer appraisal:* Individuals are assessed by their colleagues and their **line manager**.

- *team appraisal:* Team members assess their own team's performance. Feedback should preferably also come from **internal customers**, that is, employees elsewhere in the company who are clients of the team and also from a supervisor.

- *upward feedback*: Managers and others in senior positions are appraised by those who work under them.

Employees may find the introduction of 360-degree feedback both **threatening** and challenging. The exercise should be made as **non-threatening** as possible by focusing on strengths as much as weaknesses. **Respect for the confidentiality** of respondents' replies is vital. HR staff should help train and support individuals for their different roles in the process, as **appraiser**, **appraisee** or facilitator.

B Training options

Emma is Director of Human Resources in an Internet company. She is speaking at the induction of a group of new recruits:

'**Ongoing training** has been a key factor in the growth and development of YourNetBiz.

Initial training is carried out on arrival in the company as **induction training**. This includes an introduction to the company, its mission and history, as well as training relating to your job role and **mandatory** health and safety **training**. A lot is done internally, using informal and semi-formal methods such as **work-shadowing** of more experienced colleagues, **coaching**, **mentoring** and **buddy systems**. The necessary skills may also be obtained in other ways, through different forms of **supervision**, **on-the-job training** or self-study. **E-learning** is growing quickly, especially for some technical training and **skills updates** that lend themselves to this form of delivery.

External courses also have a place in our portfolio of training and staff development. They can be delivered by part-time study at local colleges on **day-release courses** or through university programmes that lead to professional qualifications. Individuals who want to be considered for such training need to make a convincing business case to their **line manager** to get prior approval.

Finally, we take **training evaluation** seriously, to check your understanding of the objectives of each training session and to obtain your feedback about the quality of the training.'

24.1 Complete the table by putting a tick (✔) in the right column. Use A to help you.

	Advantages of 360-degree feedback	Disadvantages of 360-degree feedback
Combined opinion gives a more accurate and objective view.		
Comments are difficult to ignore when expressed by a number of colleagues.		
It can be motivating for people who undervalue themselves.		
It can generate an environment of suspicion, unless managed openly and honestly.		
Some skills, such as leadership, are best judged by subordinates and peers rather than superiors.		

24.2 Which forms of training listed below constitute 'on-the-job' training?

self-study	induction training	skills update
coaching	shadowing	ongoing training
mentoring	day release	mandatory training
buddy systems	e-learning	training evaluation

24.3 Carly, Personnel Manager for a supermarket chain, outlines the appraisal system to a group of new recruits. Replace the words or phrases underlined with those in the box. Use A to help you.

> appraisal   appraisers   confidential   employee empowerment   facilitator
> flattened hierarchy   line manager   non-threatening environment
> online appraisal systems   peers   performance appraisal   self-assessment
> team appraisals   360-degree appraisal   upward feedback   virtual teams

'This afternoon we're going to talk about our <u>evaluation</u> system, which if done effectively, i.e. carried out in a <u>way that does not make you feel nervous</u>, can actually contribute to your sense of <u>being in control of what happens to you</u>. Our company has a <u>structure without many layers of management</u>, so we prefer to use <u>all-round evaluation</u> as opposed to the traditional top-down <u>evaluation</u>. The <u>evaluators</u> include those from your own level as well as those above and below you. First you carry out a/an <u>evaluation of your own work</u>. Then we ask your <u>colleagues</u> and your <u>immediate boss</u> to give their opinion. These appraisals, usually done through <u>a computer program</u>, are sent to a/an <u>independent person</u> who will ensure the feedback you receive is entirely <u>anonymous and respects everyone's privacy</u>. <u>Evaluations of each working group</u> are also carried out, even for <u>teams where the members communicate with each other only electronically</u>. And you'll be pleased to hear the branch managers do not escape. They are subjected to an evaluation from their subordinates known as <u>appraisal from below</u>.'

Over to you

How effective is the appraisal system currently in use in an organization with which you are familiar?

How might your managers respond to upward feedback?

25 Teams

A Tuckman

Bruce Tuckman (born 1938) has explored how teams develop, **mature** and function successfully in the workplace. He defined a process of **team development** with four (later five) stages:

- *Forming* – The team meets for the first time and individuals start to **get to know each other. Members** are keen to establish their personality and identify others they think they can **get on with. Group norms** and a feeling of **group cohesion** gradually develop. These **initial exchanges** are followed by discussion regarding the task, on ways of achieving it and on how the group will conduct itself.

- *Storming* – This stage is characterized by a **period of conflict**. Arguments may develop on priorities, working responsibilities and a range of options for getting the job done.

- *Norming* – Having established procedures, the team is ready to **get down to** productive work.

- *Performing* – The team works effectively and **gets on with** the job. **Team spirit** is high. Members **get through** their tasks more quickly and may **collaborate** to solve problems.

- *Adjourning* – (added in 1977) When the team's work is finished individuals may celebrate success but feel nervous about changes that lie ahead. They may regret losing the **camaraderie** of the group.

A manager who knows about these stages will be better able to **build a winning team** and **promote teamwork**.

B Belbin

Section 1.2

Meredith Belbin (born 1926), working at Henley Management College in England, conducted research into management teams and how they operate. It had been noticed that some teams of executives (although they contained very able individuals) **performed poorly** in teamwork and others performed well. When a business game was introduced to one of the courses, Belbin discovered that it was the contribution of particular **personality types** rather than the ability of the individuals themselves that was important to the success and failure of **teamworking**.

He identified nine useful roles that are necessary in a successful team. They can be placed into three groups: some team members make significant contributions to the *ideas* used in the team, others are able to focus on the *task* in hand and a final group concentrate on the *people* and **interpersonal relationships** within the team.

C Emotional intelligence

Chapter 1

Daniel Goleman (born 1946), developing work done by Salovey and Mayer and others, is a psychologist who has specialized in **emotional intelligence**. In his research into nearly 200 global companies, Goleman found that, while the qualities traditionally associated with leadership – such as intelligence, **toughness**, **determination** and vision – are required for success, they are insufficient. Truly effective leaders are also distinguished by a high degree of emotional intelligence, which includes **self-awareness, self-regulation**, motivation, **empathy** and **social skills**. Goleman found direct ties and a strong correlation between emotional intelligence and measurable business results.

25.1 Alexei, an MBA student, has summarized Tuckman's stages in group development. Complete his notes then number the stages to show the correct order.

.... – Group members work productively together.

.... – Individuals test their strengths and approaches to the task facing the group; disagreements and conflict may arise and have to be resolved.

.... – The group becomes more cohesive, with clearly established roles and working procedures.

.... – The group dissolves as the project ends.

.... – The early encounters between the individual members, when people do not yet know the others well.

25.2 Find five phrases including the word **get** in A that match the definitions below.
1 to start doing a task with serious effort
2 to continue doing something
3 to complete the task
4 to have a friendly relationship with
5 to become acquainted with someone

25.3 Use terms from C to complete the table presenting the five components of emotional intelligence.

Motivation	Passion to work for reasons beyond money or status. Drive to achieve
	Ability to control or redirect disruptive impulses and think before acting
	Proficiency in managing relationships and building effectiveness in leading change
	Ability to understand and respond to the emotions and reactions of other people
	Ability to recognize and understand your own moods, emotions and drives, as well as their effect on others

25.4 Head hunters Samira and Carmel are discussing what they look for in an effective team leader. Complete their conversation using expressions from A, B and C.

Samira: The i.................... e...................., when you open the conversation with a potential management candidate is very revealing, I find. If they can't establish good i.................... relationships quickly, they are not likely to get on with their team and cope with the different p.................... t.................... within any one team.

Carmel: The ones that p.................... p.................... lack flexibility in their dealings with others. We need someone who can engage well in t.................... and develop enthusiasm and t.................... s.................... to b.................... a w.................... team.

Samira: Yes, that type of leader encourages c.................... and a spirit of c.................... and friendship in the team.

Carmel: Oh yes. They need e.................... i.................... as well as demonstrating a certain degree of d.................... and 't....................' for effective leadership.

Over to you

Think about your own strengths as a team worker and write a personal statement to add to your CV.

26 Managing knowledge and learning in organizations

Learning organizations

Any organization which continuously transforms itself to be competitive is a **learning organization**. Building in **continuous learning** processes across all levels of the organization can help to improve business performance. Traditional **learning processes** simply look for errors and correct them (**single-loop learning**). A more productive approach is **double-loop learning**, advocated by Chris Argyris, in which the assumptions and goals that lead to the action are questioned rather than just adopting a short-term solution. To create a true learning organization, where both individuals and the organization itself are continuously learning, they should:

Identify all **sources of knowledge** and information, whether external (clients, suppliers, competitors) or internal (employees)

Create structures and processes for **collecting** and **sharing knowledge** and information throughout the organization

Use formal and informal development opportunities to promote a **learning environment** that produces business results

Create a **'no blame' culture** that welcomes questioning and debate and creates an atmosphere of trust

Create opportunities for individuals **to be stretched** and challenged to develop their abilities

Utilize business improvement tools to measure the learning process

Value **intellectual capital** as much as financial assets

B Knowledge management

In a large number of business sectors **knowledge management**, rather than manufacturing efficiency, is a source of competitive advantage. Peter Drucker identified the value of knowledge, not just the value of labour and capital, as vital for modern managers. **Acquiring**, **developing** and sharing knowledge is part of many managers' routine work, and is part of the process of **adding value** to a company's product or service. **Knowledge networking** can also help with innovation and new product development. The sharing of **best practice** in large and complex organizations can lead to cost reductions and innovation.

Knowledge can be in two forms:

- **Explicit knowledge** – the data and information held in databases and files
- **Tacit knowledge** – intuition, experience and judgement.

Companies now have **talent management and retention** schemes to ensure they keep the advanced **research expertise** and **technical skills** that some of their **high flyers** have acquired.

26.1   Make nine noun phrases from A and B with the key word **knowledge**.

26.2   Join the two halves of the sentence and create definitions of the words in the box.

continuous learning	double-loop learning	learning environment
learning organization	learning process	no-blame culture

1	The procedure for	a	the whole of one's working career.
2	Acquiring knowledge over	b	by reflecting on the appropriateness of the original goals and assumptions.
3	Situation or setting where	c	learns and transforms itself through providing learning opportunities for individual members.
4	A company or entity that	d	groups are more interested in solving problems than finding out who was responsible for the mistake.
5	A set of attitudes where	e	acquiring knowledge is encouraged and facilitated.
6	The process of correcting errors	f	acquiring knowledge.

26.3   Complete this abstract for a talk to be given by Marina Rubio, expert on HR management, using terms from A and B.

With almost one-third of companies now operating a formal talent strategy, anyone with any interest in HR management will be aware of the significance of this concept in terms of organizational b.................... p.................... . Organizations have recognized the need for continuous investment in the i.................... c.................... of their staff to generate competitive advantage. This has placed increased pressure on HR to demonstrate their a.................... v.................... and justify investments as 'business critical'.

Following the recent recession, many organizations have revived their attempts to r.................... and attract the h.................... f...................., by putting t.................... m.................... firmly back onto the executive agenda. Investing in the right people and s.................... their capabilities is once more a key focus for HR.

Programmes originally focused on the top talent but then came the recognition that everyone needs to realize their full potential; the result of this has been a blended approach to talent management. Many organizations focus on managing selected subgroups, such as graduate populations and those with r.................... e.................... .

Based on research carried out by the Chartered Institute of Personnel and Development, this paper demonstrates recent trends in the development of talent m.................... .

Over to you

Reflect whether double-loop learning could be employed to improve the learning process in your organization.

What types of knowledge add value to your department? How can they be shared and networked within the organization as a whole?

27 Leadership

A Transactional and transformational leaders

In the past decade there has been a **paradigm shift** in leadership theory, as writers such as Burns, Alveoli and Bass have described the characteristics of **transactional** and **transformational leadership**. According to these theories, transactional leadership is based mainly on rewarding good performance or punishing unsatisfactory performance, sometimes known as **contingent reward leadership**. Some managers only intervene when a subordinate fails to meet expectations: this **passive** approach is known as **management-by-exception**. Other managers may even adopt a **laissez-faire approach**, avoiding intervention. However, **active** transactional managers will take steps to avoid poor performance. Transformational leadership is a **participative** leadership style, in which the leader provides:

1 **Individualized consideration** – listening to **followers'** concerns, considering their needs and **fostering self-development**

2 **Intellectual stimulation** – **challenging assumptions** and **nurturing creativity**

3 **Inspirational motivation** – communicating clearly and persuasively a vision that will inspire their followers

4 **Idealized influence** – Providing a **role model** which will gain respect and trust. Followers know that their leader will apply consistent, **impartial rules** in any conflict.

These concepts have been used in the design of **leadership development programmes** in which managers are encouraged to move from passive approaches to active transactional and transformational approaches.

B Is there a difference between leadership and management?

Dr White, a lecturer in leadership studies, is introducing a new module:

The **'great man' theory** based on the concept that leaders are born and that leadership cannot be taught has now been discredited. However, there is wide acceptance that certain **personality traits** can be helpful in potential leaders. Warren Bennis has carried out research into the characteristics of leaders in many different environments. According to Bennis, good leaders have **integrity** and are trusted by their colleagues; they are **risk takers** who are willing to experiment; they have **a clear vision** which they translate into reality and a passion which helps them to achieve their objectives. Bennis found that how they **deal with adversity** is a most reliable indicator of successful **charismatic leaders**.

The career of Ernest Shackleton, the Antarctic explorer, is a case study of leadership in action. In planning the expedition, Shackleton demonstrated considerable skill as a manager. He recruited a talented and **well-balanced team**, with relevant skills and experience. He ensured that the expedition was **suitably equipped** with the right **resources** for such a challenging expedition. **Teambuilding activities** helped to **create strong bonds** between the different personalities as the *Endurance* sailed south.

When their ship became stuck in ice, Shackleton's **leadership qualities** emerged. He had **a clear focus** on his ultimate goal and was prepared to **take risks** when necessary to ensure the survival of the whole team. He kept everyone busy and **set a** strong **personal example** of the sort of behaviour he expected. He was able to **manage conflict** with sensitivity when it arose among members of the team and his **fairness** to everyone, his **charisma** and **communication skills** were evident to all. It was thanks to his leadership qualities that the whole crew eventually returned to safety, nearly two years later.

27.1 Match the expressions on the left with their definitions on the right.

1	impartial	a	a way of interacting with followers that involves them in making decisions and generating ideas
2	integrity	b	a person whose behaviour sets an example that other people like to follow
3	paradigm shift	c	not favouring one person over another, always fair
4	participative leadership style	d	honesty and strength of character
5	role model	e	a fundamental change in the model or theory on which we base our understanding of something

27.2 Before a group of managers attend a leadership development programme, their subordinates are asked to fill in a questionnaire on their management style. Use expressions from A to fill in the gaps in the questionnaire to label the types of management style that the statements relate to. The first one is done for you.

Management style

<u>Contingent reward</u>: the person I am rating works out agreements with me on what I will receive if I do what needs to be done.

❖ .... management-by-exception: they focus attention on mistakes and deviations from what is expected of me.

❖ .... management-by-exception: problems have to be critical before the person I am rating will take action.

❖ Non-leadership:....................: my manager avoids getting involved when important issues arise.

❖ .... leadership:

Inspirational motivation: In my mind this person is a symbol of success and accomplishment.

❖ ....: they introduce new projects and new challenges.

❖ ....: they listen to my concerns.

❖ ....: I am ready to trust the person to overcome any obstacle.

27.3 Dr White asks his group to answer the questions: to what extent did Shackleton illustrate Warren Bennis's leadership traits? To what extent was he also a good manager? Use the words in the box to write your own short answer. The first sentence is given to you below. Use the information in B to help you. Compare your answer with the sample answer in the answer key.

charismatic leadership	clear vision	create bonds	deal with adversity
fairness	integrity	managing conflict	personality traits
resources	risk taker	team-building activities	well-balanced team

From the case study it is evident that the explorer Ernest Shackleton demonstrated many of the <u>personality traits</u> identified by Warren Bennis in his research …

Over to you

According to Warren Bennis, 'Managers do things right. Leaders do the right thing.' What does this statement tell us about the difference between leadership and management?

28 Managing across cultures

A Hofstede

Cultural diversity is becoming a significant management issue because of factors such as globalization and an increasing number of cross-border partnerships. Based on his experience at IBM, Geert Hofstede developed a framework for understanding **cultural differences** and managing problems that can arise because of lack of **cultural awareness**. He identified four dimensions for defining work-related values associated with national culture:

- *Power distance* – the way people perceive power differences and how a society handles inequalities and differences in status
- *Individualism/collectivism* – behaviour towards the group
- *Masculinity/femininity* – behaviour according to characteristics associated with the genders
- *Uncertainty avoidance* – the need for structure and clear rules.

The framework is used to help determine the suitability of certain management techniques for various countries. For example, in a country with a small power distance such as the USA, managers find it natural to **delegate responsibility** and employees will **accept responsibility**. This would not be the case in a country with a larger power distance, such as Mexico, but employees there might accept more discipline.

B Cross-cultural competence

Johan, who works for a consultancy firm that specializes in cross-cultural training for multinational organizations, is introducing a workshop:

'Training in cultural awareness is a vital element in the development of the global managers of the future. Apart from the cultural differences that we can see between countries, you need to be aware of the **cultural impact** of working in different business sectors and different functional roles. How people in an organization act towards each other, deal with customers, approach their work, even how they dress, can be very similar and fit the organization's **values**, beliefs and the **norms** that are shared by all staff.

Senior managers have responsibility for setting the **corporate culture** and influencing the way members of staff behave in the workplace. As managers move from one country to another and encounter different functional areas of management, it is imperative that they get away from a restricted '**silo' mentality**, from **cultural stereotypes** and from any **cultural assumptions** they have made.

During this workshop I hope we can explore some of the ways in which people from different organizational or geographical cultures can have very different norms, **unwritten rules** and **codes of behaviour**.'

C Cross-cultural differences

Going to work in the Gulf state of Qumran for the national oil company was quite a **culture shock** after my previous career as an HR manager in the retail sector in Stockholm. The company provided a substantial briefing on the **cross-cultural competences** of an international manager as part of the induction programme as soon as I arrived in Qumran.

For the first few months I thought I had moved **out of my comfort zone**. I had to get used to differences in **dress code**, gestures and **body language**. Attitudes to time and punctuality were very different from those I had been used to in Scandinavia. Management meetings and negotiations also followed very different rules. Socializing with colleagues and the line between family life and working life was different. And of course the **prevailing culture** in the oil company meant that I encountered very few women in senior management roles.

28.1 Find eleven collocations in A, B and C using the adjective **cultural** or the noun **culture**. Then use six of these to complete the description of the benefits of this training course.

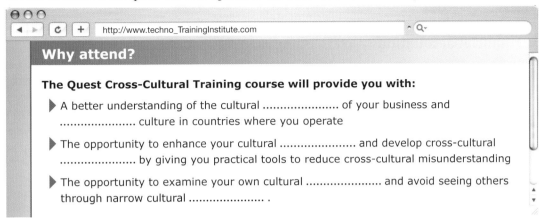

Why attend?

The Quest Cross-Cultural Training course will provide you with:

▶ A better understanding of the cultural .... of your business and .... culture in countries where you operate

▶ The opportunity to enhance your cultural .... and develop cross-cultural .... by giving you practical tools to reduce cross-cultural misunderstanding

▶ The opportunity to examine your own cultural .... and avoid seeing others through narrow cultural ....

28.2 The sentences below are from the findings of a study of different countries. Add the countries to the appropriate categories in this table.

Small power distance	Large power distance
More individualist	More collectivist
Strong uncertainty avoidance	Weak uncertainty avoidance
More masculine values	More feminine values

a In the UK the prevailing culture expects people to develop and display their individual personalities, whereas in China people are defined and act mostly as part of a long-term group, such as an age group or profession.

b In New Zealand employees generally relate to one another as equals and managers delegate responsibility, unlike Malaysia, where subordinates tend to acknowledge hierarchical positions and do not expect to accept responsibility.

c In the USA assertiveness and competitiveness are considered valuable qualities, whereas in the Netherlands warm relationships and quality of life are given priority.

d UK workers are comfortable to take risks and change jobs frequently, whereas Japanese workers like to work in a structured situation and remain with the same company.

28.3 Match the dictionary definition to the correct term/s from the box.

codes of behaviour/norm/unwritten rules	comfort zone	'silo' mentality	values

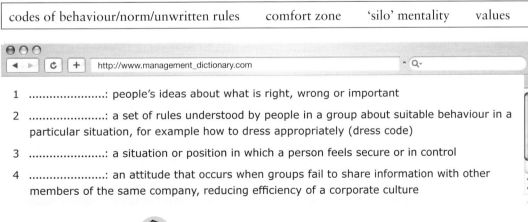

1 ....: people's ideas about what is right, wrong or important

2 ....: a set of rules understood by people in a group about suitable behaviour in a particular situation, for example how to dress appropriately (dress code)

3 ....: a situation or position in which a person feels secure or in control

4 ....: an attitude that occurs when groups fail to share information with other members of the same company, reducing efficiency of a corporate culture

Over to you

What are the main points you would include in a presentation about cross-cultural issues for people coming from abroad to work in your country?

29 Financial accounting and management accounting

A Financial accounting

Financial accounting is about measuring the performance of an organization and communicating this to the external stakeholders. These include **shareholders**, who have an **equity stake** entitling them to a share of the profits, and **creditors**, such as banks who have loaned money and suppliers who provide goods. Financial accounting can answer such questions as: what is the company worth? Are its shares a profitable investment? Can it pay back all the money that it owes?

Accounting is more than just recording transactions in the form of **debits** and **credits.** That activity is known as **book-keeping**. A much bigger picture is required to understand the interaction of all the factors affecting the organization's financial position. Each organization issues an **Annual Report**, a public document distributed to shareholders, in which the management discusses the past year's performance and presents the company's accounts. These consist of **financial statements** representing the organization's financial activities in different ways. The **balance sheet** balances all the **assets and liabilities** of the business to show the **net worth** of the company at a particular moment in time. The **profit and loss account** (or **income statement**) shows **revenue**, expenses and the **net profit** or loss over a specific period of time. The report also includes a **cash flow statement** detailing the flow of funds from the company's operations, investments together with financing activities, such as selling shares or borrowing to raise capital. When a company has a **positive cash flow** it can pay out **dividends** to its shareholders. If there is a **negative cash flow**, even a profitable company may fail because it cannot meet its short-term obligations.

B Management accounting

Management accounts are issued regularly for internal use and include detailed information and **forward projections** for the financial year, to help in **budgeting** and **cost control**.

Managers use this information to help them examine the profitability of individual products or services. They can conduct a **break-even analysis** of individual products, to discover at what level of production costs are just covered by income. They can calculate the **gross margin** for each item, that is the margin of profit between the price that it is sold for and the **direct costs** of producing it, such as raw materials, and the **contribution margin** of each unit to the company's general costs or **overheads**. These are **indirect costs**, such as the cost of maintaining a telephone helpline, and may include both **fixed costs**, such as the rent for the premises and **variable costs**, which increase if production is increased.

To help identify all these different factors, management accountants **allocate costs** to an individual product line or use **cost centres** to evaluate parts of a company separately, for example, the research and development unit. A **profit centre** takes this a step further by making a unit of the organization function like a small business, controlling its own costs and profit-generating activities.

Another method of allocating costs is by **activity-based costing (ABC)**, based on identifying the **real cost** of each activity, including its associated overheads. For example, a software manufacturer might find that 80% of the calls taken by its helpline concern a particular product. They may decide to withdraw or improve the product, to reduce the costs of dealing with the calls.

29.1 Here is part of the balance sheet for a group of charity shops collecting and selling furniture to help homeless people. Decide if the items gapped are **assets** or **liabilities** for the charity. Note that **debtors** are people or organizations that owe money to the organization.

Fixed	Equipment	93,200			
	Vehicles	8,700			
				101,900	
Current	Cash	11,020			
	Stock	3,750			
	Debtors	1,750			
			16,520		
Current	Creditors		9,000		
	Working capital			7,520	
					109,420
Long-term	Capital	80,000			
	Net profit	5,286			

29.2 Find nine terms in B using the base word **cost**.

29.3 Match the two halves of the statements.

1	To check if the company can afford to pay out a **dividend** shareholders would	a	a **cost-control** programme to improve future net margins.
2	To decide if it is worth buying shares to obtain an **equity stake** in a company, prospective investors might look at	b	its book-keeping, recording payments to and from its accounts (debits and credits).
3	Before deciding to stop manufacturing a product, management would carry out	c	the company's **forward projections** in the **management accounts**.
4	A financial manager might decide to introduce	d	set up **profit centres** in individual units.
5	To set a **budget** for their spending in the next year, a management team might look at	e	look into the **direct costs**, or **overheads** and the **contribution margin**.
6	A small company will employ an external accountant to oversee	f	look at the company's **cash flow statement** to see if there is a **positive cash flow**.
7	To make departments manage their costs more efficiently, the company may	g	a **break-even analysis** to find the gross margin of the product.
8	To decide if a new product line would increase revenue, managers would	h	the bottom line of the **balance sheet** in the **Annual Report** to find the **net worth** of a company.

Over to you

Find the Annual Report of an organization you are interested in online. Try to answer the questions at the end of the first paragraph in Text A.

30 Business valuation and interpretation of accounts

How much is a business worth? A case study in valuation of assets

A private company owned four hotels in Scotland. The owners decided to sell the company to an international hotel chain. How could they decide a **fair price**? The simplest method of **business valuation** might seem to be to balance the assets and **debts** of the company to find its net worth. However, assets are reported in the balance sheet at **book value**, that is, the amount the asset cost to buy, less its **depreciation** over time. In this case, one of the hotels is in a prime tourist location, Princes Street, Edinburgh, so the current value is a great deal more than its **historic cost** indicates. **Fair value** accounting would take this into account.

Instead, the buyers could base the valuation on the projected **free cash flows** of the company, using the **discounted cash flow** method. In this case, the **net present value** (**NPV**) could be calculated using an estimated **discount rate**. This rate is based on the concept of **the time value of money**, which takes into account the fact that money may be worth less over time. If your grandfather put £100 in an envelope fifty years ago and gives you those notes today, the gift would be worth much less than its original value.

Finally, the two companies decided to use the **market comparables** approach. As the hotels were sold as **a going concern**, the fair price was easy to agree by comparison with other similar sales advertised in the property market. In fact, the international chain paid slightly more than the **market value**, because acquisition of the Edinburgh hotel completed its goal of having a hotel in the principal street of every European capital city and would generate a high **return on assets**.

A shareholder's perspective

When deciding to buy shares in a company, shareholders' first concern is the income they will receive: their **return on investment** (**ROI**). They will compare this with the benefits and risks of other competing investments. Then they might compare the **Price/Earnings** (**P/E**) **ratio**, that is, the current share price divided by the earnings in the last twelve months, with those of similar companies in that sector.

Financial analysts compare company performance with that of similar organizations, on behalf of potential shareholders. They use **financial ratio analysis** to highlight:

- **Profitability** – how has revenue exceeded expenses? This can be measured by ratios such as the **gross profit margin** (profit made from buying and selling stock) or by the **return on capital** (**ROC**) invested in the business.

- **Short-term liquidity** – how easily can cash and other assets meet liabilities? This can be measured in terms of the **working capital ratio** or **current ratio** (current assets over liabilities), which shows the ability of a business to pay its short-term debts.

- **Long-term solvency** – the company's ability to meet its long-term obligations. Analysts will compare the company's **solvency ratio** with the typical ratio for that industry. This is a measure of the company's after-tax income (allowing for depreciation) and its total liabilities. A ratio less than 20% would be cause for concern, whatever the type of business.

30.1 MBA student Susie Leung summarizes the case study in A. Replace the underlined expressions with terms from A.

An international hotel chain decides to purchase four hotels, including one located in a prime UK tourist spot, which it believes would provide generous <u>earnings from its assets</u>. The vendor sells the hotels as a <u>successful business that will continue to make profit</u>. Making <u>an estimate of what the company is worth</u> was not a simple task. Not only had the cost of its assets been noted <u>at the original cost of buying them, less a reduction over time</u>, but also the vendors were not taking into account the fact that <u>money has less value over time</u>. The concept of <u>the value of a business or asset compared to the present prices of other similar businesses</u> was used to arrive at a final, more realistic price, which was slightly higher than <u>that of other similar properties on the market</u>. This is <u>an approach which benchmarks the value against other similar items sold in the same market</u>. Another approach they could have considered uses the projected <u>amount of money the company would have after it has paid all its expenses</u>, and applies a time-related <u>reduction percentage</u> to estimate <u>what the business is really worth now</u>.

30.2 Susie and her classmate Kaoru are comparing two telecoms companies from the point of view of two financial advisors comparing how to invest their client's money. Complete their dialogue, using terms from A and B.

Susie: Look at Easiphone – its .... margin is really high, but its current ratio is low.

Kaoru: Is that the same as the .... ratio?

Susie: Yes. Look, it has liabilities of £80 milllion but its assets are only £50 million. It would have a problem with .... liquidity.

Kaoru: I agree. It might not be able to pay its ....

Susie: So its .... isn't as good as it looks. Did you check the .... ratio?

Kaoru: Yes, if you take off tax and ...., that ratio is only 16% – it doesn't look as though Easiphone will be able to survive in the long term.

Susie: So far we think Easiphone is not likely to give shareholders a good .... on investment. What about Youtalk?

Kaoru: Well, I think there is a better ROC, that's the return on the .... that has been invested in the business.

Susie: And the investors think it's pretty healthy, too: I checked out the .... ratio on Youtalk and if you divide the share price by earnings from the year 2010, the market value of the shares has really gone up.

Kaoru: So, those investors must think their earnings are going to increase in the future. I suppose .... *(Easiphone/Youtalk)* would be the best one to invest in.

Over to you
To find out more about financial analysis search for articles on www.businesslink.gov.uk

31 Banking and financial services

A Zopa and the banks

There seems to be a storm brewing in **financial services** about the use of services such as Zopa, the online lending exchange where **depositors** can **lend money** directly to **borrowers** at a mutually agreed **interest rate**. Dubbed the 'eBay of banking', the idea behind Zopa is that, by cutting out the big banks, borrowers should get cheaper rates, and lenders get higher returns. The **APR (Annual Percentage Rate)** paid by the borrower consists of the rate set by the lender plus Zopa's initial fee.

With banks setting strict **lending criteria**, many consumers have been turning to Zopa as a source of credit. Zopa attributes its uniquely low **bad-debt** rate to its risk-management system, using **credit rating** agencies, such as Experian, also known as **credit bureaux**. These carry out **credit searches**, analysing data about individuals or companies to assign a **credit score** based on the applicant's **credit history**. Some commentators also believe that the direct relationship between borrowers and lenders in this online **social marketplace** creates an atmosphere of mutual trust.

B Applying for a bank loan

When it receives a **loan application**, the bank considers the **creditworthiness** of the owners, the amount and purpose of the loan and how the business can generate sufficient cash to meet the **repayment schedule**.

Banks require guarantees of **security** for a loan, for example, an asset supplied as **collateral** that the bank can sell if the loan is not repaid. The bank may impose a **debt** covenant, an agreement setting conditions during the loan period. For example, the borrower agrees to maintain a certain level of working capital or not to pay out dividends until the **maturity** date, when the loan is finally repaid. If the borrower **defaults** on the repayments or breaches the covenant, the lender can demand immediate repayment and take possession of the collateral.

C Cash management services and payment products

Marcus Sehr, head of global transaction banking, Deutsche Bank, writes about current trends:

'Today, most payments are executed via **electronic transfers**. This trend affects every walk of life, from individual consumers paying at a shop via **direct debit** to an importer transferring money to an exporter's account via a cross-border **credit transfer**. Today's payment products involve **customized solutions** designed to help control the timing and conditions of payments. To speed up international payments, the new **clearing system** of the Eurosystem **Central Banks** allows cross-border transactions to be processed in real time.

By centralizing negative and positive balances into a single account position on a daily basis, overall liquidity can be improved, creating opportunities for the short-term investment of any **surplus funds**. Rapid access to payment information can be accessed through channels such as **SWIFT**, a system used for secure exchange of data. Banks also need information to prevent **money laundering** and **fraud**.'

31.1 Without looking back at the texts, brainstorm seven terms formed from the base word **credit.**

31.2 Complete these FAQs from an online financial service provider aimed at young entrepreneurs, using four of the terms from 31.1 and other words from A, B and C.

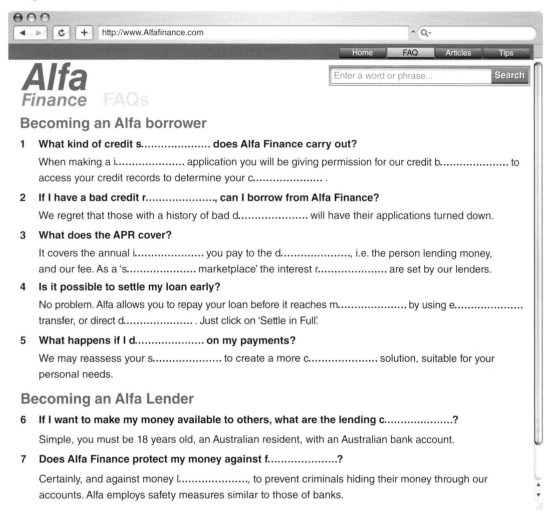

Becoming an Alfa borrower

1   What kind of credit s..................... does Alfa Finance carry out?

When making a i..................... application you will be giving permission for our credit b..................... to access your credit records to determine your c..................... .

2   If I have a bad credit r....................., can I borrow from Alfa Finance?

We regret that those with a history of bad d..................... will have their applications turned down.

3   What does the APR cover?

It covers the annual i..................... you pay to the d....................., i.e. the person lending money, and our fee. As a 's..................... marketplace' the interest r..................... are set by our lenders.

4   Is it possible to settle my loan early?

No problem. Alfa allows you to repay your loan before it reaches m..................... by using e..................... transfer, or direct d..................... . Just click on 'Settle in Full'.

5   What happens if I d..................... on my payments?

We may reassess your s..................... to create a more c..................... solution, suitable for your personal needs.

Becoming an Alfa Lender

6   If I want to make my money available to others, what are the lending c.....................?

Simple, you must be 18 years old, an Australian resident, with an Australian bank account.

7   Does Alfa Finance protect my money against f.....................?

Certainly, and against money l....................., to prevent criminals hiding their money through our accounts. Alfa employs safety measures similar to those of banks.

31.3 Match the term (1–5) to the correct definition (a–e).

1	clearing system	a	Restrictions placed on the borrower by the bank.
2	collateral/security	b	Providers of banking, insurance and investment products.
3	covenant	c	How authorized banks or other financial institutions settle payments at the end of each trading day, transferring money from the payers' to the payees' accounts.
4	financial services	d	Money remaining after all liabilities and taxes have been paid.
5	surplus funds	e	Properties or assets providing security to the lender in case the borrower fails to pay back the loan.

Over to you

Visit www.swift.com. What do the letters SWIFT stand for? What services might SWIFT offer a company you know in doing cross-border business?

32 Raising finance – equity and debt

A Venture capital and private equity

Companies need to raise money for a variety of purposes. Most people think of money being required for **business start-ups**, but there are other stages in the development of a company where capital is required. For example, **second-stage financing** provides working capital for initial expansion once the company is established and **bridge financing** may be needed to supply capital for growth in the period when a private company is preparing to **go public** and make an **IPO (initial public offering)** of its shares on the **stock market.** In **equity financing**, investors buy shares in the **stock** (that is the capital originally put into the business). This is why shares are also commonly referred to as **stocks**.

People often think about **venture capitalists** as **business angels**, wealthy entrepreneurs who provide capital in return for a share in the company ownership. However, a larger proportion of **venture capital** is provided by **investment banks**, which specialize in finding appropriate sources of capital, and by **private venture capital partnerships**. In return for an equity share, these groups offer capital, particularly to young companies in the fields of new technologies or those with an innovative **business model**. They may even provide **seed financing** for the initial costs of setting up a company, such as preliminary market research. Governments may also provide **grants** to assist company start-ups.

B A good business plan

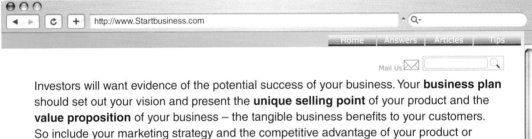

Investors will want evidence of the potential success of your business. Your **business plan** should set out your vision and present the **unique selling point** of your product and the **value proposition** of your business – the tangible business benefits to your customers. So include your marketing strategy and the competitive advantage of your product or business model. Most importantly, show that you have done the financial planning by including **sales forecasts** and **projected cash flows** and balance sheets for at least three years ahead. You also need to identify **performance milestones**: specific objectives to be achieved as the company develops. This is important because investors are often unwilling to release all their funds at once but prefer to issue a **first tranche** of the equity investment at the beginning and a **second tranche** when certain milestones have been met.

C Debt or equity financing – Microsoft and Manchester United

Dr Gao is introducing a lecture on capital structure:

'Microsoft Corporation recently sold $2.5 billion of its debt to investors and Manchester United football club made a **debt offering** of £500 million. Why would such iconic companies choose to take on debt rather than issuing equity shares?

In considering their **debt to equity ratio,** companies need to **trade off** the risk of **bankruptcy** (which makes the debt less attractive to investors) against the advantage that interest payments on debt are **tax-deductible,** in contrast to dividend payments.

The required **return on equity** is usually higher than the interest on debt. For existing owners, raising money through a share issue will involve diluting ownership, reducing the return on individual shares. By issuing debt **securities** such as **bonds** and **notes,** the firm has fixed payments and doesn't give away a share of the profits. **Bondholders** and **noteholders** are patient people: repayment on Microsoft's new note offering is due in February 2041!'

32.1 Managers of a new DVD rental and download company seek financial advice. Match the items in the two columns to create a dialogue. Use A, B and C to help you.

1	Tell me first, what's the unique selling point of your product?	a	We're thinking of approaching investment banks or private venture capital partnerships.
2	Sounds like a good deal. Now, what is your main source of financial backing?	b	We offer free rental for every 10th DVD rented or downloaded.
3	What is your plan for revenue generation and giving real value to customers?	c	But would we risk becoming bankrupt if we can't make the interest payments?
4	I can see from your business plan you have an attractive business model. What about second-stage financing?	d	Our value proposition is offering movies in many different languages, giving customers huge choice at low cost.
5	Well, before approaching them, review your sales forecasts and performance milestones for the next 3 years.	e	... and get less profit as owners. And maybe lose some control over the way we run our business.
6	Of course, you realize investors may release only the first instalment of the loan initially?	f	Initially our savings, with a small government grant as seed funding.
7	But looking at your plan, I don't think these projected cash flows are very realistic.	g	Yes, and a second tranche after reaching the next milestone which is £3.6m turnover for 2013.
8	Yes – you could also issue debt as long-term bonds. The interest you pay to the bondholders will reduce your tax bill.	h	Financial planning is not our strong point. What do you think about offering shares to the public in an IPO?
9	You have to trade off the risks to get a sensible debt to equity ratio. Remember, you will have to pay dividends on shares ...	i	Yes. Our first milestone is achieving 20% of the UK market, and the second is gaining 5% of the European market.

32.2 Complete the article using terms from A and C.

Harley-Davidson Stocks Roar Ahead

Investor Warren Buffett yesterday purchased $300m worth of d.................. o..................
from the struggling motorcycle manufacturer, Harley-Davidson. The v.................. capitalist,
who already owns s.................. in US giants General Electric and Mars, is seeking to capitalize
on the current economic crisis. Along with other n.................., Buffet will receive 15% interest
on the debt s.................. . Although this high interest rate will cut earnings to 18 cents a
share, the s.................. market reacted positively to this show of confidence from the famous
business a.................. and Harley's shares rose by over 15%.

Over to you

Think about a particular stage of development in a company you know. What is capital needed for? What combination of debt and equity might be appropriate to raise funds?

Read some case studies about business funding in the Starting Up section of the UK government website, www.businesslink.gov.uk

33 Mergers and acquisitions

A Value creation and synergy

The purpose of any commercial company is to create value for its shareholders. For example, when two powerful insurance companies Norwich Union and CGU **merged**, they **re-branded**, adopting the name Aviva plc and the slogan: 'One Aviva, twice the value'. This added value, the difference between the value of the combined company and the sum of the original values of the stand-alone companies, is known as **synergy**. The main aim of **mergers** and **acquisitions** (**M&As**) is to add shareholder value through synergies which are measurable in terms of cost savings or revenue generation.

In mergers, two companies create a new entity and issue new stock to their shareholders, whereas in an acquisition one company ceases to exist and is integrated into the acquiring company or held as a **subsidiary**. There are various ways for companies to combine. Competitors in a market where there is **overcapacity** can create synergy through **horizontal integration**. This allows economies of scale, such as larger orders to suppliers, and cost cutting, such as closing plants. Companies may also cooperate through **joint ventures** and **strategic alliances**, agreements that do not require a change in ownership.

Companies with an existing business relationship, such as suppliers and producers, can increase value through **vertical integration**: for example, a car manufacturer buying a component firm or a chain of car showrooms. In **market-extension mergers**, companies selling the same products in different markets can merge to access more consumers, while those with related products in the same market can join in **product-extension mergers**. In **conglomeration**, companies with no common business area form a diversified group to reduce risk.

Merger waves are periods of increased acquisition activity, often associated with a **boom** in the value of the stock market in a country or business sector. The recent wave of **cross-border M&As** may be part of a strategy for overseas market penetration, such as UK-based Vodafone's **takeover** of Ghana Telecom.

B Implementing M&As and post-merger integration

M&As have economic effects, so many countries have **competition** or **anti-trust laws** to prevent a small number of companies from dominating the market and engaging in **anti-competitive practices**. Managers and their professional advisors must exercise **due diligence**, investigating all the risks and legal issues involved. They will check the financial health and prospects of the target business to be able to value it. In an acquisition, the buyer will usually pay a **premium** above the market value of the company in order to gain control representing some of the potential synergies from the deal.

After a merger or acquisition, company operations and practices need to be **re-structured**. **Post-merger integration** concerns not only practical aspects like pricing strategies and integrating IT systems but also retention of key people. In the knowledge economy, the 'return on talent' is an important part of value creation. Effective post-merger strategies aim for an outcome where the 'best of both' is represented, or **a transformational approach**, in which the two merging companies change into something much stronger than either of them had been before – the 'best of both plus'.

33.1 Find eight 2- or 3-word combinations from A and B containing these words: **merger/s, acquisition/s, integration.**

33.2 Complete this student's notes on examples of how synergy is created by adding the names of the types of mergers, acquisitions or company collaboration the examples represent. Use A to help you.

1 .... integration: in 2002, budget airline EasyJet took over Go! because of overcapacity in the holiday industry.

2 ....-extension merger: in 1998, Chrysler Corp. merged with Daimler Benz to form DaimlerChrysler, giving Chrysler an opportunity to reach more European markets and Daimler Benz greater presence in North America.

3 .... integration: Walt Disney Corporation paid a premium to acquire Pixar Animation Studios in 2006 when there was a boom in the market for animated films.

4 .... (or .... alliance): Sony Corporation and Ericsson set up a separate company, with 50:50 investment to develop and manufacture mobile phones, combining Sony's consumer electronics expertise with Ericsson's technological leadership in the communications sector.

5 ....: during the 1980s, General Electric also moved into **financing** and **financial services**, acquiring subsidiaries in these fields, which in 2005 accounted for about 45% of the company's net earnings.

33.3 Complete the article about a key player in the merger implementation process, using words from A and B.

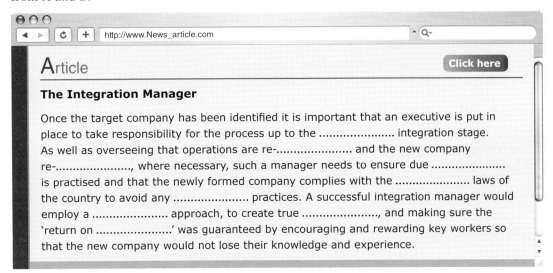

○ ○ ○

◄ ► C + http://www.News_article.com ^ Q▾

Article

Click here

The Integration Manager

Once the target company has been identified it is important that an executive is put in place to take responsibility for the process up to the .... integration stage. As well as overseeing that operations are re-..................... and the new company re-....................., where necessary, such a manager needs to ensure due .... is practised and that the newly formed company complies with the .... laws of the country to avoid any .... practices. A successful integration manager would employ a .... approach, to create true ...., and making sure the 'return on ....' was guaranteed by encouraging and rewarding key workers so that the new company would not lose their knowledge and experience.

Over to you

Find an online report of a recent merger or acquisition. Decide if it involved horizontal or vertical integration or conglomeration. What sort of synergy do you think was created for the companies involved?

34 Corporate governance

A Company ownership and the principal–agency problem

The simplest type of ownership is a **sole proprietor** owning a small business. Sole proprietors can lose personal assets if the business fails, so they may register as a **private limited company** (**Ltd.**). This means that the company becomes a **legal entity**, with **liability** limited to the amount of capital the owners have invested in the company. However, when a company becomes a **public limited company** (**plc**), allowing its shares to be traded on the stock market, the problem arises that ownership and control are now separated. The **directors** are agents, or **fiduciaries**, legally responsible for making the best use of the shareholders' money. How can the shareholders, the **principals**, ensure that their agent will look after their investment? Directors might use **inside information** about the company's financial condition to act for their own benefit against the interests of shareholders – as occurred most famously in the Enron scandal, where shareholders lost nearly $11 billion as a result of fraud by the **executives**.

Solutions to this problem include strict regulation by government and industry bodies. For example, under **the Companies Act**, registered UK companies must hold an **AGM** (**Annual General Meeting**), where shareholders can vote on important issues. Company accounts must also be impartially reviewed by **external auditors**. If they are satisfied that the accounts are true and fair, auditors will give an **unqualified opinion**. A **qualified opinion** suggests the accounts are inaccurate or incomplete.

B Executive compensation

CEO **compensation** in the USA rose from 42 times that of an average worker's wage in 1982 to 531 times as much in 2000 and people often claim that this is unfair. However, to avoid a **conflict of interest** it is necessary to reward executives well. Such **remuneration** schemes include **bonuses** based on key performance indicators or **share options** allowing them to buy company shares at some future date, at a fixed price, thus making a profit if the company performs well. However, often these **incentives** are designed so that they promote a fixation on short-term success, which may encourage the type of risk-taking that led to the 2008 banking collapse.

C The board of directors

*These extracts from the UK Financial Reporting Council Corporate Governance **Code** explain the roles and responsibilities of boards of directors and shareholders:*

Corporate governance is the system by which companies are directed and controlled. The shareholders' role is to appoint the directors and auditors and to satisfy themselves that an appropriate governance structure is in place. The **board of directors** has **collective responsibility** for setting the company's strategic aims, supervising the management of the business and reporting to shareholders on their **stewardship**.

There should be a clear **division of responsibilities** between the running of the board and the **executive responsibility** for running the company's business. The **chairman** is responsible for leadership of the board and ensuring its effectiveness. The **non-executive directors**, who are not employees of the company, have the role of constructively challenging proposals on strategy. The board has ultimate **accountability** for risk management and ensuring **transparency** in communicating with investors.

34.1 Complete these terms related to corporate governance, choosing from the box.

a legal entity	a private limited company	a public limited company (plc)
a qualified opinion	a sole proprietor	an unqualified opinion

1 .... is an individual who owns a small business.

2 .... is a company whose owners or shareholders are not liable for the company's debts and can lose only the amount of money they have invested in the company.

3 .... is an independent auditor's judgement that a company's financial statements are fair and in accordance with accounting regulations.

4 An organization that is .... has the same status under the law as an individual person: it can enter into a contract, be sued if it fails to meet its contractual obligations or prosecuted if it commits a criminal act.

5 .... is a company which offers shares for public purchase. It must have a minimum of share capital (over £500,000) and can be listed on the London Stock Exchange, where shares can be traded freely amongst investors.

6 .... is a statement by an auditor that information included in a company's accounts is not complete or that the accounting methods used do not follow accounting regulations.

34.2 Complete this extract from an MBA textbook using terms from A, B and C. The first letter of each term has been provided.

The Role of the Board

According to the UK c..................... of c..................... g....................., shareholders have the role of appointing the b..................... of d..................... . These directors are f....................., that is agents on behalf of the shareholders, with c..................... responsibility for the success of the company and a..................... for its failures. In other words, they must demonstrate good s....................., taking care of the company for which they are responsible and always showing openness, or t....................., towards their p....................., the shareholders. The board should include non-e..................... directors, responsible for ensuring that objectives are reached. Supervising the effectiveness of the board is the c..................... . The d..................... of responsibilities between the chairman and CEO should be clear to avoid any potential c..................... of interest, given the amount of i..................... information to which they have access.

Election of the board is carried out during the A..................... G..................... M....................., which serves as a forum for shareholders to elect or remove the chairman, question the board's decisions, raise issues of the fairness of executive c....................., where necessary, and appoint the e..................... a....................., accountants from a specialist accounting company who check the company's balance sheet.

Serving on a board involves some amount of r....................., which can take the form of i..................... to stimulate performance, such as b....................., extra payments directly related to performance, or s..................... o..................... which link e.....................' wealth to that of the company. In all their activities, the directors and shareholders are responsible for conforming to the national laws such as the C..................... A..................... (UK) and its equivalents worldwide, such as the US anti-trust laws.

Over to you

Access online the annual report of a company you are familiar with. What issues were raised at the Annual General Meeting?

35 Risk management

A Risk management and financial planning

A manager in the treasury department of a multinational telecoms company talks about the work of his department:

'**Mitigating risks** in operations and in our cash management is an important responsibility of the **treasury department**. One of our important functions is to manage the company's debt requirement, for instance, through issuing bonds.

Another important part of our **risk management strategy** is **hedging**, that is protecting future borrowing costs or foreign exchange **exposure**. For example, we might budget to spend dollars in the USA later this year. By then, the **exchange rate** will have changed, as currency markets are very **volatile**. So we buy **reserves** of foreign **currency** to mitigate that risk.

We play an integral role in the strategic planning process in terms of adding value and improving **capital efficiency**. Because we are a telecoms company, we are a **regulated company** and have an **operating licence**. This means we are obliged by the government to provide certain services. For example, we might be obliged to build ten mobile phone masts, but one is very remote and will be used very little compared to city locations. It may take ten years to pay for itself. By standard valuation techniques, such as net present value (NPV), this may not seem an efficient use of capital. However, we have to take into account the **tangible** and **intangible benefits** – our **brand reputation**, for example. The bottom line is we want people to buy our products and invest in our shares.'

B Risk management and investment

The first rule of investing is 'Don't put all your eggs in one basket'. **Diversification**, having different types of assets or investments in different regions or sectors, is important. However, it is difficult for small investors to **spread** their **risks** without specialist knowledge of the market. This has led to the development of funds. These **investment vehicles** include **pension funds** that manage the investment of the money employees are saving for their retirement and **mutual funds**, which allow investors with small amounts of capital to access professionally managed, diversified **investment portfolios** of different types of equities, bonds and other securities. Investors can choose the level of risk they are willing to take. **Hedge funds** are a more sophisticated form of investment run by private investment partnerships that use more flexible investment strategies. They operate under less regulation and aim for high returns but they are very dependent on the fund managers' expertise and are considered riskier than mutual funds.

Some investors prefer to put their beliefs before simple profit. This has led to funds which operate on the principles of **Islamic banking**, and the rise of **ethical investment**, which avoids investments detrimental to health, the environment or world peace.

35.1 An MBA student introduces his seminar group to the Heat Map. Complete his explanation. Use terms from A and B to help you.

A heat-seeking approach

Annualized earnings at risk for disguised global financial-services company, $ million

Risk concentration
▬ High (>10% of capital)
▬ Medium (>5% of capital)

	Business unit							
	A	B	C	D	E	F	Other	Total
Total market risk[1]	55	275	25	10	15	5	10	395
Credit risk[2]	150	350	125	625	40	N/A	N/A	1,290
Operational risk	30	210	30	150	10	2	N/A	432
Business-volume risk	80	270	60	275	25	5	5	720
Total earnings at risk	315	1,105	240	1,060	90	12	15	2,837

[1]Includes equity-market and interest-rate risks.
[2]Includes lending, investment, and counterparty risks.

'A Heat Map is a simple tool prepared by the t.................... department to demonstrate not only the e.................... to possible risks for each business unit but also overall corporate earnings that are at risk. It uses colour to show areas of high risk, with red showing the more v.................... areas, accounting for 10% of the company's capital at risk, in this example. From this a risk profile is drawn up and the board of directors devises an appropriate r.................... strategy. Where the company has an investment p...................., there may be a need for d.................... to s.................... the risk. Risks can also be m.................... by h...................., for example, holding a currency r...................., in case there are changes in the e.................... rate. Companies r.................... by the government are not always free to act as they wish, but must factor in the costs of fulfilling the terms of their o.................... . Companies also have to weigh up not only the t.................... benefits of certain risk-management strategies, such as capital e...................., but also the i....................: for example, investment in safety measures in car design might be expensive, but enhances b.................... .'

35.2 Complete these definitions of terms from B.
1 An investment .... is a means of investing money.
2 A .... fund is a stock of funds collected from a group of people and invested in securities including stocks and bonds.
3 .... banking is a system that allows investors to share profit and loss while avoiding collection and payment of interest.
4 .... investment is a system based on the investor's personal moral principles.
5 A .... fund is often set up as a private investment partnership, open to a limited number of investors and requiring a large initial minimum investment over at least a year.

Over to you

Think of the risks a major retailer and an international telecommunications company are exposed to.

Now look at the annual reports for two real companies and assess their risk-management strategies. Publically listed companies will provide copies of the annual report on their website.

36 Managing in difficult times

A A year that changed the world

Archive

In March 2008, there was panic on **Wall Street** after respected private equity firm Carlyle Capital admitted that it could not repay its debt. For every $1 of equity, the $22bn Carlyle Capital Corporation fund was **leveraged** with $32 of loans. In other words, it toppled over under the weight of unsustainable debt. A process that would bring Wall Street and the world's banking system to its knees had begun.

In September, Lehman Brothers, America's fourth-largest bank, collapsed. Lehman's 5,000 London staff turned up to work on Monday to find their employer was **bankrupt**. They left carrying their belongings in boxes. Lehman Brothers had a huge commercial property loan book, specializing in **sub-prime debt**. These were high-risk **mortgages** issued to US borrowers with low incomes. The lenders gambled on the buyer's income increasing to keep up the repayments. Worse still, Lehman, along with many other institutions, had **securitized** this risk in the form of **derivatives**, secondary financial products traded on the markets whose value depended on the value of these risky assets. A whole **shadow banking system** had come into existence, borrowing and lending money without the **regulation** and **checks and balances** of the traditional banks.

Fearing a **bank run** on the UK's largest mortgage lender HBOS, the UK government agreed to **waive competition law** to allow Lloyds Bank to take over HBOS. Meanwhile, on the other side of the Atlantic, the world's biggest insurance company, AIG, saw its stock market value collapse. If the firm went under it could bring the world banking system down, so the US **Federal Reserve** announced an $85 billion emergency loan. By October the world's financial system had come closer to absolute collapse and long-term **recession** than at any time since the 1930s.

The continuing effects of the financial **meltdown** threatened entire countries in a **sovereign debt crisis**. By 2011, the Irish government had to be bailed out by the EU to save the country and its banking system from economic collapse, following a 36% fall in the **housing market**.

B Capital markets and the credit crunch

After the collapse of two US investment banks and the near collapse of AIG, **interbank lending rates** rocketed. **The London Interbank Overnight Rate (LIBOR)** is the rate at which banks across the world lend to each other – the lower the rate, the more accessible cash usually is. It is a measure of confidence between banks. Most lenders tap into this commercial market to help fund their daily operations.

A major cause of the **credit crunch** was the shutting-off of money to commercial markets as financial companies retained cash to protect themselves against losses from **bad debts**. The US government announced a $700 billion programme to buy up **toxic assets** from endangered US institutions. **Central banks** of governments around the world have also helped the global **capital markets**, through **quantitative easing**, creating money by buying securities, but they cannot guarantee that the cash will filter down to smaller financial institutions which need it most to avoid collapse.

One solution is **bank capitalization** that has larger **equity buffers** and is less dependent on debt and leverage. However, once banks become '**too big to fail**' and governments **underwrite** them, there is less incentive for the banks to move to a safer capital structure.

36.1   MBA student Alex Manning is preparing an essay on the credit crunch of 2008. Help him organize his thoughts by putting the terms and expressions from the box in the right place in his table. Some have already been done for you.

The Credit Crunch of 2008: how did it happen, who was involved and what measures can be used to tackle these problems?

> ~~bad debts~~   bank capitalization   ~~bank run~~   bankrupt   capital markets   ~~Central banks~~
> ~~checks and balances~~   credit crunch   ~~derivatives~~   equity buffers   Federal Reserve
> interbank lending   The London Interbank Overnight Rate (LIBOR)   meltdown
> ~~mortgages~~   quantitative easing   recession   regulation   sovereign debt crisis
> sub-prime debt   toxic assets   underwrite   waive competition law   Wall Street

Type of investment products and lending	derivatives, mortgages,
Institutions and markets involved	Central banks,
Things that went wrong	bad debts, bank run,
Ways of tackling the crisis and making banks safe	checks and balances,

36.2   Complete the dialogue between two MBA students following a lecture on the 2008 credit crunch, using the terms and expressions in the box.

> checks and balances   leverage (×2)   securitizing   shadow banking system
> sovereign debt crisis   sub-prime   too big to fail   underwriting

Casey: So, did you understand what really caused the credit crunch? I'm not sure that I did.

Ashraf: Well, I get the impression it was .... that caused the problem.

Casey: You mean people were using borrowed money to borrow more money?

Ashraf: Yes. So as well as the real banks with all their elaborate systems of ....
that they use to avoid risky lending, there was also a whole .... of other
companies lending and .... risky products.

Casey: So what you mean is they were turning these things like .... mortgages
into securities to sell on the markets?

Ashraf: Exactly, and the banks were buying them up. The problem with .... is that
the loss is greater to the investor when things start to go wrong; in reality they are
unable to sustain the debt. However, as the banks were ...., governments
had to bail them out and buy up their debts.

Casey: The lecturer called that ...., I think?

Ashraf: Yes. And of course some governments like Greece and Iceland couldn't pay their
debts, so that's when the .... came about.

Casey: Oh, OK, I think I've a better understanding of it all. Thanks, Ashraf.

Over to you

What do you think are the future trends in the times in which you will be managing? Find some websites to explore one of these themes:

- The growth of the BRIC countries: Brazil, Russia, India and China
- Islamic banking
- Ethical finance

37 Strategic options

Porter – competitive forces

Michael Porter identified five factors affecting the **competitive position** of a company arguing that a company must take account of these **competitive forces** in the wider industry scene before it can make decisions about the best strategy for its future success.

Based on this model, Porter identified three **generic strategies**:

- **competing on price**
- **differentiating** products and services by offering something not offered by competitors
- focusing on a **niche market**.

Later, he went on to consider the role of **diversification** as a strategy. A sixth force was also added to Porter's original model: **complementors** – products that sell well with another product, or make it easier to buy or use, for example, computer software and hardware.

Ansoff – product development versus market development

Strategic marketing objectives are set in terms of which products to sell in which markets. Igor Ansoff developed this four-way matrix to identify strategies a company can adopt:

	Existing products	**New products**
Existing markets	**Market penetration**: focus on increasing brand loyalty of existing customers and attracting new customers in that market segment	Product development: develop new products for existing customers, especially where companies' strengths depend on a close relationship with these customers
New markets	**Market development**: persuade customers in different market segments or geographical regions to buy the company's existing products	Diversification: develop new products for new markets. This is the most risky strategy, as the company has to move outside its **core competencies** to acquire new skills and invest in new resources.

Case study: the world watch industry

29

In 1948, the Swiss watch industry had 80% of worldwide sales. By 1985 this had dropped to just 13%, with new entrants to the market, the Japanese, having taken over as **market leader**.

The Swiss had failed to recognize the **shift in consumer demand** towards cheaper, electronic rather than mechanical watches. By adopting new manufacturing technologies and **positioning themselves** in a **competitive cost position**, the Japanese had established themselves in the increasingly important American and Asian markets.

The fight-back by the Swiss watch industry focused on product innovation and design, **high volume sales** and **aggressive marketing**, most notably in the USA, where Swatch's diversification programme aimed at making the company a total fashion enterprise. The Swatch, a blend of Swiss and watch, launched as a response to Japanese competition, is now a classic case study in **strategic marketing**.

37.1   Match the words in columns A and B to make nine word combinations from A, B and C.

A			B
aggressive	generic	competencies	position
bargaining	market	entrants	power
competitive	niche	leader	products
core	potential	market (x2)	strategies
existing	substitute	marketing	

37.2   Complete the case study on the global automobile industry.

Let's consider the c..................... of companies within the global automobile industry. While suppliers of auto parts are plentiful, they are not considered a threat in terms of profit. In fact, from a s..................... point of view, some of their products could be regarded as c..................... to be marketed alongside the cars. However, other suppliers of inputs to the car industry, such as organized labour, can be a powerful force. Buyers (auto dealerships, car rental firms and individual consumers) remain unorganized but can negotiate on price. Competition amongst e..................... car firms further strengthens the customer's b..................... . Successful m..................... is costly, which means there is little threat from n..................... to the market. There is little cause for concern with regard to s....................., as despite alternatives – motorbikes, bicycles, public transport – most people prefer to purchase their own car. So there is unlikely to be a s..................... in the foreseeable future. However, r..................... within the industry itself is particularly intense, resulting in highly a..................... campaigns. There is a h..................... but oversupply occurs due to enlarged production capacity, while d..................... proves difficult, except in n....................., such as sports cars: d..................... into new markets has fairly limited potential. As a result of such c....................., the auto industry bears only moderate profits.

37.3   Use the information in the case study of the automobile industry in 37.2 to summarize Porter's five forces model in the table below.

Force	Strength of force (rating: *low, moderate, light, high*)	Comment and trends
Buyers		
Suppliers		
Substitute products		
Potential entrants		
Rivalry		

Over to you

Choose an industry that you are relatively familiar with and conduct Porter's five-force analysis. Where are the key competitive pressures in your industry? For example, suppliers may have a strong bargaining position and be able to set prices, or buyers may have a wide choice and may easily be able to switch between one organization's products and another's.

38 Analysis

A   Gaining competitive advantage through corporate strategy

Managers in every type of organization need to devote considerable attention to the **corporate strategy** that can drive the business. They need to monitor factors in the **near and far environments** that may affect their own organization, and make appropriate plans to manage these. One definition of corporate strategy is the way a company **creates value** for its customers, employees and investors through its **configuration** and through the **coordination** of its **multimarket activities** (its configuration in terms of product, geographical and vertical divisions).

The organization's **mission statement** is a useful starting point for setting realistic objectives and making **strategic decisions**. Good mission statements identify the organization's **core values**, indicate the products or services that it provides and the **critical factors for success** in the marketplace where it operates.

B   Mission, tactics and operational planning

The **strategic planning cycle** provides managers with a structure that allows them to set the organizational purpose and its current strategy and consider how the organization's resources can be best utilized.

Driven by the mission statement, senior managers can create a **corporate plan** that provides the overall direction for their business and influences the tactical and **operational plans** that can be created for individual parts of the organization. **Tactical plans** support strategic plan implementation and achievement of tactical goals. They are more specific and concrete than strategic plans and focus on intermediate **timeframes**, usually one to three years. Operational plans, on the other hand, support the implementation of tactical plans and achievement of operational goals, with timeframes of below a year.

The corporate plan needs to be closely linked to the **external environment** in which the organization operates and should take into consideration the culture as well as the strengths and weaknesses within the organization. A **situational analysis** should be carried out, including a general audit of the types of **environmental factors** influencing the performance of the business and the forces operating in the **competitive environment**. Many organizations now prepare **contingency plans** that can help them prepare for dramatic change in their business environment. They will also carry out a SWOT analysis where the understanding of the external environment is specifically related to the organization and its **internal environment**.

C   Scenario planning

In today's climate of rapid social and technological change, strategic decisions can be increasingly difficult to make. **Scenario planning** is a strategy instrument that can help senior managers make well-informed decisions about the long-term future of their organization and assist **forward planning** in a complex environment. It differs from market research or financial **forecasting techniques** in that it depicts alternative 'futures' instead of just projecting **current trends** forward. This enables organizations to model a series of potential futures and to modify their future plans according to the most feasible scenarios. Scenarios are not **predictions** but **plausible hypotheses** of various 'what if' possibilities.

38.1 Refer to B and label the diagram below using the terms in the box. Then add an appropriate time scale for the second and third stages of the cycle.

operational goals   operational plans
strategic goals   tactical goals   tactical plans

Top management
Organization-wide perspective

Middle management
Departmental perspective
Timeframe: ....

First-level management
Unit/individual perspective
Timeframe: ....

Strategic planning cycle

38.2 Complete the dictionary definitions below by choosing the correct term from the box.

contingency plan   core values   corporate strategy   multi-market activities
scenario planning   situational analysis   strategy investment   value creation

http://www.business_onlinedictionary.com/

1 Principles that guide the functioning of an organization, both internally and in terms of its relationship with the outside world.

2 A planning strategy involving visualizing the consequences of possible future events and how the organization could respond to them.

3 A management goal whereby the interests of customers, investors and employees are taken into consideration to ensure a successful business or product.

4 Identification of the position of a company within its business environment and how well it meets the demands of that environment.

5 A fixed procedure for evaluating a long-term plan of action for achieving a particular goal.

6 Actions to ensure that immediate follow-up steps are taken in the event of an emergency that seek to both limit damage and maintain continuity of the organization's key operations.

7 When companies operate in a range of different product or geographical areas of business.

8 The direction and scope of an organization over the long term to meet the needs of the market.

38.3 Read the mission statement and analyse it in terms of their core values and the critical factors for success in the particular marketplace in which the organization operates.

Our vision is to be earth's most customer-centric company; to build a place where people can come to find and discover anything they might want to buy online. In meeting their needs everything we do must be of high quality. We must constantly strive to reduce our costs in order to maintain reasonable prices. Customers' orders must be serviced promptly and accurately. Our suppliers and distributors must have an opportunity to make a fair profit. (Amazon: Corporate FAQs)

Over to you

Use some 'what if?' questions to identify some significant factors an organization with which you are familiar may have to consider in its business environment.

39 Managing change

A

Planning for change with force field analysis

Organizations face constant **pressures for change** from both outside the organization and from within. **Force field analysis** is a **management tool** devised by Kurt Lewin to examine the **driving forces** that are pushing for change, and the **restraining forces** that are opposing it, thus creating an **equilibrium**, which is the existing situation. The **force field diagram** represents the **variables** involved in planning and implementing a programme for change. The existing situation is in the middle, with the forces driving and opposing change listed on either side. The diagram below illustrates the forces operating in a Xerox copier plant in the USA. By assigning a score to each force, from 1 (weak) to 5 (strong), managers can assess the relative importance of these factors and identify the **key players** in the situation. Among these will be **allies** supporting a decision and **opponents** who may have **vested interests** in maintaining the **status quo**. Managers can influence these target groups and reduce **opposition to change**.

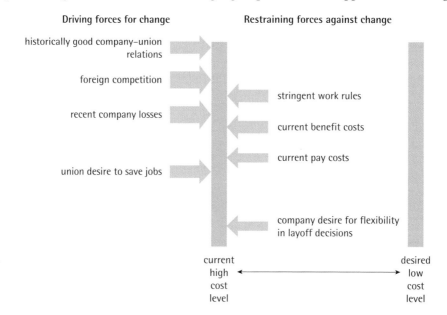

Driving forces for change

- historically good company–union relations
- foreign competition
- recent company losses
- union desire to save jobs

Restraining forces against change

- stringent work rules
- current benefit costs
- current pay costs
- company desire for flexibility in layoff decisions

current high cost level ←→ desired low cost level

B

Overcoming resistance to change

Why do more than half of change programmes fail? Why do employees often engage in **active** or passive **resistance** to change? Kotter and Schlesinger identified four main reasons for **resistance to change**:

- **Self-interest**: concerns about the effect the change will have on ourselves and anxiety about our ability to learn new skills and behaviour
- Misunderstanding: when we do not understand the implications of changes, because of inadequate communication or lack of trust
- **Inertia** and low tolerance of change: we are afraid to take a risk and leave our **comfort zone**
- We disagree with the reasons behind the decision to make the change.

Approaches to dealing with opposition to change in the workplace include effective communication, involving employees in the change effort and offering support during the **transition period**, as they **come to terms with** the need for change. Managers can also negotiate, offering incentives to employees, or use **co-option**, by inviting the leaders of the resisters to participate in the change effort. Managers may use **coercion**, with threats of job losses. Recently, researchers have pointed out that resistance to change is not a negative force, but a constructive phenomenon **that acts as a catalyst** for change. By listening to the **valid concerns** of their employees, managers can strengthen commitment to the eventual changes.

39.1 After a lecture on managing change, match the lecturer's responses (a–f) to the student's questions below (1–6).

Please can you clarify the meaning of:

1 vested interest

    a It's the actual resistance to change, our tendency to keep going in the same direction.

2 status quo

    b Think about it simply as the current or existing state of affairs.

3 'variable' in a management context

    c It's people who support us when others are trying to oppose our ideas.

4 allies

    d This represents the personal stake that underlies someone's desire to maintain or influence an action.

5 equilibrium

    e These are factors that are subject to unknown changes.

6 'Inertia' in a business context

    f It's a state of balance.

39.2 Complete the case study about managing change, using terms from the box.

allies	come to terms	driving	force field	key players	management tool
opponents	opposition/resistance	pressure	restraining	status quo	vested interest

Faced with .... for change, in the form of serious overseas competition, Xerox set a goal of reducing manufacturing costs at its New York copier plant through outsourcing certain electrical components, thus eliminating 150 jobs. The .... in the situation were the workforce. It might be expected that they would be .... of change as they had a .... in maintaining the .... to keep their jobs. However, the company had a history of good relations with their workforce, so union leaders and managers became ...., working together to overcome the .... to change. The diagram on the opposite page shows the major .... and .... forces. Union leaders and management studied ways to save money, which finally led to eliminating certain healthcare benefits. In return, the company promised no layoffs for three years. By reducing these..................... forces, changes were agreed on which reduced cost levels without eliminating jobs. This case study illustrates how .... analysis can be applied as a .... to help employees to .... with change.

39.3 Read the case study and then answer the questions using the words in brackets to help you.

A company decided to implement PAN, a new software package. IT employees argued strongly that PAN was inappropriate. The CEO's failure to listen to these valid concerns gave rise to conflict between IT and those in administration who would be using the software.

The admin department looked into an alternative application, Zeus. Representatives from both departments were invited to a product demonstration and allowed to raise questions. IT employees asked about technical specifications, while admin staff enquired about the different accountancy facilities offered by the package. It was agreed that Zeus would provide a viable solution.

1 What form did the IT workers' resistance take? (*active resistance, passive resistance*)
2 How did the product demonstration help employees to accept change? (*a catalyst*)
3 Were the IT employees co-opted or coerced into accepting the new application? (*co-option, coercion, come to terms with, resister, comfort zone, strengthen commitment*)

Over to you

Describe a change situation in which you have been or are involved. Use a simple force field diagram to identify the driving factors and resisting factors, plus their relative strengths.

40 Action planning

A Implementing strategy – management by objectives

Management by objectives (MBO) starts with clearly defined strategic organizational objectives expressed in mission and **vision statements**. To support the mission, the organization needs to set clear goals and objectives, which then **cascade** down from one organizational level to the next until they reach everyone.

Critics of MBO have pointed out that **rigid** objectives may be a source of weakness, as a modern company needs to be flexible to survive. However, MBO has evolved in line with modern management thinking. Its **overarching premise** is that of **empowerment**. Taking responsibility for performance and seeing how achievements affect the organization as a whole increases motivation and loyalty.

B SMART objectives

Peter Drucker, in his book *The Practice of Management*, proposes the SMART **acronym** to make MBO more effective. The idea of SMART is to set goals that are **attainable** and for which people feel **accountable**. Drucker said that goals and objectives must be:

- Specific
- **Measurable**
- Agreed (relating to the participative management principle)
- Realistic
- Time related

Notice that the 'A' in SMART is 'agreed'. This is sometimes referred to as '**achievable**' but it is not enough for the goals and objectives to be set at the top and then cascaded down. They must **trickle down** through various stages of agreement. The only goal that is going to be met is one that is agreed on.

To create a mechanism for **monitoring progress** towards the agreed goals you need a clear path marked by **accountability** checkpoints. Remember **the participative principle**: rewarding goal achievers sends a clear message to everyone that **goal attainment** is valued. After this five-stage process, the cycle begins again, with a **review** of the strategic corporate goals in the light of performance.

C Resource allocation

Resource allocation is a central management activity for strategy implementation. However, **organizational politics** may prevent resources from being allocated effectively to particular divisions and departments. Structural reorganization may be required, as new strategies often place emphasis on different areas of the business.

There are practical considerations in allocating resources. **Contingency mechanisms** allow for changes in the organization's situation. Items are given **priority rankings** to decide which should be funded if more resources become available or dropped if funds have to be reduced. Sometimes this prioritization is done by means of **algorithms** or by **decision-making software**.

40.1 Look at the case study and analyse it against Peter Drucker's SMART objectives acronym.

> Serious traffic congestion and flooding of the local river in the business district of a large city in Malaysia meant that an Icelandic firm was contracted to build an 8.9 km tunnel to divert floodwater away from the city centre. They would also provide a two-tier motorway system above the tunnel, to relieve congestion. The construction firm consulted with local teams and together agreed solutions to resolve excavation issues in the construction of the tunnel. The tunnel was completed in 2007, on time and within budget. The flow of traffic is dramatically reduced and floodwater has since been successfully diverted from the business district.

40.2 Complete this description of how the management team of a call centre reviewed their objectives at the end of the MBO cycle. Use terms from A, B and C.

> Initially, in order to achieve our v...................... statement we tried to implement Drucker's M...................... p...................... by setting p...................... goals and rewarding employee contribution. We had hoped that these objectives would t...................... d...................... down to those dealing directly with the callers. However, we soon realized that the goal of finishing calls within seven minutes was not being met; calls were becoming more complex or there was a faulty new product, and operators were finishing calls early to meet targets, leaving customers frustrated. So we considered a contingency m...................... . We gave call types priority r...................... depending on the problem presented by the caller. We also reassessed resource a...................... and took on more staff to handle the calls. By m...................... p...................... , we had picked up the shift in the goal environment and goals were changed accordingly. We also built in accountability c......................, where the staff could decide for themselves if the caller's needs had been met or refer them to a supervisor. This e...................... staff and helped them to feel a...................... for their decisions. We learned that you can't just c...................... decisions downwards, you need participation and empowerment: after all, that is the overarching p...................... of MBO.

40.3 Match the meanings (1–4) to the correct terms from B and C.
1 A computer application that goes through the process of selecting a logical choice from a set of available options.
2 A set of rules to be followed to enable someone to solve a problem.
3 A word formed from the first letters of a group of words making up a name.
4 The pursuit of self-interest within a company while showing total disregard of its effect on the efforts of that company to achieve its goals.

Over to you

What are the objectives of MBO? What do you think may be its disadvantages?

Allocating resources can be a political activity in firms that do not use strategic management. Why is this true? Does adopting strategic management assure easy resource allocation? Why?

US English terms

UK English term	US English equivalent
AGM (Annual General Meeting)	Annual Meeting
agree an annual budget	agree on an annual budget
analyse data	analyze data
assessment centre	testing center
behaviour	behavior
business angels	private investors
centre	center
charge subscriptions	charge subscription fees *or* charge for subscriptions
competency profiling	skill assessment
contract of employment	employment contract
credit bureaux	credit bureaus
critical factors for success	critical success factors
cross-border mergers and acquisitions	international mergers and acquisitions
diffuse	penetrate
early majority	core adopters
fit for purpose	appropriate
followers	subordinates
grade	level ("Staff at different levels.")
guidance notes	help notes
have a propensity to	have a propensity for + -ing (e.g. "Have a propensity for innovating.")
high flyers	up-and-comers *or* up-and-coming employees
induction programme	hiring program *or* training program
induction training	new-employee training
industry bodies	trade bodies *or* industry associations
Late majority	late adopters
lead users	lead customers
licence	license
near and far environments	immediate and long-term environments *or* short- and long-term environments
object of desire	desired object
order books	orders booked
overheads	overhead
permanent posts	permanent positions
pre-employment checks	reference checks
preventative action	preventive action
prioritise risks	prioritize risks
procurement department	order department
profit and loss account	profit and loss statement *or* income statement
programmes	programs
recruitment and selection process	hiring process
referees	references
reporting channels	reporting lines
research brief	research parameters *or* research assignment
search engine optimisation	optimization
secure investment	obtain investment
selection panel	selection committee
services	service ("He works in service.")
sifting	sorting
skills updates	skill updates
sole trader	sole proprietorship

sources of finance   sources of funding
stages of adoption   adoption stages
statements of account   account statements
take charge of   be in charge of
task in hand   task at hand
terms of reference   terms of agreement
trade directories   business directories
treasury department   the accounting department
waive competition law   waive anti-trust laws
white goods   major appliances

Answer Key

1.1   allocate resources
cover costs
identify needs
measure performance
make a profit
meet targets
pay attention to detail
report on results
set prices
spot opportunities

1.2   Interpersonal roles
> Figurehead – Performing symbolic duties as a representative of the organization
> Leader – Establishing the organizational culture and motivating the staff
> Liaiser – Developing and maintaining business networks

Information roles
> Monitor – Collecting all types of information that are relevant and useful to the organization
> Disseminator – Communicating information from outside the organization to relevant groups inside the organization
> Spokesperson – Communicating information from inside the organization to outsiders

Decision-making roles
> Entrepreneur – Spotting opportunities, being innovative and championing change in products, services or business processes
> Disturbance handler – Dealing with unexpected challenges and crises
> Resource allocator – Deciding on the most appropriate use of the organization's resources
> Negotiator – Negotiating with individuals and dealing with other organizations

1.3 **1** Being able to make a <u>profit</u> is really only a tiny aspect of business. <u>Interacting</u> with experts from the various fields of management as well as <u>collaboration</u> with other students taught me to challenge my <u>assumptions</u> of the role of management. Amongst other things, the course gave me a practical insight into soft management skills as well as helping to <u>develop</u> my creative <u>thinking</u> skills.

     2 I now have a better idea about <u>managerial</u> work in general. As a marketing manager, I was able to <u>integrate</u> my previous experience with marketing. In addition, <u>discussion</u> of the more <u>complex issues</u> of psychology during the course means that I am now much better at <u>identifying</u> and meeting the <u>needs</u> of my customers. I also learnt how to become a much more effective <u>communicator</u>.

     3 The part time Executive Programme gave me the chance to put the theory into practice immediately. I am responsible for <u>setting</u> and <u>meeting</u> production targets for a small electronics firm. I learnt about the different management <u>responsibilities</u>. This knowledge has made it easier for me to stick to an agreed <u>budget</u> for production and to apply key performance <u>indicators</u> to monitor performance more accurately.

     4 Not only did I learn how to become a team <u>player</u>, but I was able to develop my own personal <u>leadership</u> skills. And by the end I had become a much more effective <u>communicator</u>. I'm far from becoming a <u>figurehead</u>, but I do have much more confidence and have applied for management jobs in several different <u>sectors</u> of <u>industry</u>. I hope that soon I'll be able to <u>mentor</u> a junior member of staff and put it all into practice.

2.1

Term	Definition
chain of command	Handing decision making from the higher levels of an organization to lower ones
lines of responsibility	The specification of individual employees' responsibilities for particular aspects of work and of their management responsibilities and who they report to in the organization
spans of control	The number of people a manager can effectively manage in a particular situation
'managerial mystique'	When managers behave as detached unemotional experts who do not need to share their ideas or explain what is going on to the people who work for them
subordinates	People who are below a manager in the hierarchy
collective leadership	When decision making and authority is shared by a group of managers
bureaucratic organizations	Where there are fixed and formal rules and policies which must be followed with little freedom for individuals to make their own decisions
entrepreneurial culture	A business environment encouraging new ideas and individual effort
Board of Management	A committee of members elected by the shareholders to manage and oversee the company

2.2 1 **Functional** – Departments are separated according to the different aspects of company work, such as producing goods or dealing with the financial matters.

2 **Multi-divisional** – The company is divided into separate units specializing in a particular area of the world or has separate units dealing with particular types of products.

3 **Matrix** – The company uses a mixture of divisional structures, to enable it to be more flexible and organize its work around specific projects.

4 **No formal structure** – Very small companies run by a single person or group are like this.

5 **Flat** – In this type of structure responsibility is shared, with fewer managers and with individuals being responsible for their own tasks.

6 **Product** – the organization is divided according to a particular product or type of product, each of which has functional teams to take care of staff, finance, etc.

2.3

chain		command
layer	of	management
line		responsibility
span		control

3.1 administrative management, scientific management, management by objectives, industrial management, general management, modern management, management consultant, management theory, management concept, management guru

1 management guru
2 management consultant
3 scientific management
4 management concept
5 administrative management

3.2 Managers must examine the organization's <u>macro</u> environment and draw up <u>strategic</u> plans for the organization's response to what is likely to lie ahead.

Managers must build up the <u>strategic</u> plan of the organization and put in place procedures which can help with the preparation and implementation of plans.

Managers need to <u>motivate</u> and set an example for their staff, as well as clarify the <u>roles</u> and <u>responsibilities</u> of the organization's teams and individuals.

Managers need to ensure that the work done by the various teams and departments is consistent with the overall plan for the organization.

Managers need to ensure that what happens is what should happen, in accordance with the organizational plan.

3.3 1 Production <u>processes</u> at the turn of the twentieth century across Europe and the USA benefited greatly from the <u>principles</u> of the <u>scientific</u> theory of management, based on research into <u>mass</u> production which dealt with optimum <u>productivity</u> rates and resulted overall in greater <u>efficiency</u>. Production <u>targets</u> were set for individuals according to the time available and the <u>share</u> of the workload. Applying these principles enabled Ford to <u>capture</u> the major share of the automobile market at the beginning of the twentieth century. The man who developed these theories was <u>Frederick Taylor.</u>

2 <u>Knowledge workers</u> are those who develop and use knowledge in the workplace. Along with the <u>decentralization</u> of the role of management, these are just two of the concepts that can be attributed to one person in particular, <u>Peter Drucker</u>.

3 The manufacturing and <u>service</u> industries as well as the <u>public</u> sector have gained from a greater understanding of the roles of management, and the separate functions involved in management, as highlighted in the <u>seminal</u> work of <u>Henri Fayol.</u>

4.1

Noun	Adjective	Noun	Adjective
competition/competitor	competitive	privacy	private
correction	corrective*	public	public
entrepreneur	entrepreneurial	society	social
finance	financial	strategy	strategic
institution	institutional	sustainability	sustainable

* Note there are two adjectives from correct: correct = something is right /corrective = making something right

4.2 1e, 2a, 3f, 4b, 5c, 6d

4.3 1 We don't hold <u>equity</u> and so our <u>mission</u> as a <u>social</u> enterprise is to generate financial <u>resources</u> to facilitate the operation of our association.

2 <u>Planning</u> a schedule for the <u>volunteers</u> who run our <u>non-profit</u> <u>organization</u> is not a simple task; while we don't have a problem finding people willing to <u>donate</u> their time free of charge, they are not necessarily available when we need them. Luckily, we also have a group of <u>waged</u> staff working specific shifts to ensure a permanent presence. They all agree it's highly <u>satisfying</u> work.

3 Being <u>accountable</u> to our <u>shareholders</u> is a necessary evil for any private enterprise. It is vital that we provide them with an annual report, outlining the amount of <u>profit</u> generated over each 12-month period, as well as our positioning compared to that of the current <u>competitors</u> in the market.

5.1

Verb phrases	Noun phrases
access data analyse (raw) data collect data	data mining raw data amounts of data software package database software time management software proprietary software

5.2 1 proprietary software

2 transaction

3 logistics

4 inventory control

5 stock

6 shelf space

5.3 Suszanna is the project manager and Markus the junior consultant.

Markus: Sorry to disturb you, I'm trying to make sense of these terms. Could you just confirm a few things for me before I <u>sign</u> <u>off</u> this contract? I know the daily <u>rate</u> depends on my <u>grade</u> but I'm not sure of the rest.

Suszanna: Well, basically, the <u>terms</u> of <u>reference</u> are set out by our company, as the consultancy firm, and you can use our <u>time</u> management <u>software</u> to keep track of the hours you do.

Markus: OK, I understand. What if I'm working <u>off-site</u>; what am I entitled to?

Suszanna: The usual, accommodation and travel but also any incidental <u>expenditure</u>, such as internet fees and photocopying. So make sure you keep all your receipts.

Markus: I'm sure I'll lose some of them from time to time. Do I need to send <u>invoices</u> to the clients?

Suszanna: No. Send them to me and I'll download a <u>statement</u> of <u>account</u> and the invoices and send them to the client for payment.

5.4 1 Family and friends can always be of help by providing <u>funding</u> for a <u>start-up</u> business. Stelios Haji-Ionanou, for example, had access to $20 million in funding, thanks to his family's shipping business. This is how he was able to fund the loan to set up EasyJet, a major European low-cost airline.

2 <u>Grants</u> may be available in some areas to encourage innovation and to attract inward investment. Local enterprise agencies will be able to help you to identify these potential <u>sources</u> of finance and to discuss the criteria for eligibility.

3 Unlike grants, <u>loans</u> have to be paid back. It is worth trying different banks and finance houses to find out what is available. Lenders will normally require some form of <u>collateral</u>, such as property, as a guarantee that the borrower will pay back the loan.

4 If you're lucky, you may be able to identify <u>business angels</u>: people who will help to fund the business, usually in return for a share of the business or its profits.

5 Then there's <u>venture</u> capital – this is another source of private equity. Providers are seeking to invest other people's money and expect their investment to have paid off within seven years.

6 Finally, if none of these options is available, entrepreneurs may even consider using their own private <u>savings</u> to fund a small business venture.'

6.1 1 They are good at spotting <u>trends</u> in the macro environment and don't just accept the <u>status quo</u>.

2 Almost everyone takes <u>risks</u> and is prepared to gamble with their time, commitment and money.

3 They are flexible and willing to experiment with their <u>initial</u> <u>concept</u> to make it work.

4 They utilize their sense of <u>creativity</u> to the benefit of the company and have a <u>propensity</u> to know exactly when to <u>innovate</u>.

5 All of them recognize the need to <u>commercialize</u> their innovative product or service and ultimately achieve competitive <u>advantage</u>.

6.2 1e, 2a, 3d, 4i, 5b, 6g, 7c, 8f, 9h

6.3 Essential to the success of any industry is <u>innovation</u>. <u>Innovation</u> pushes the boundaries in <u>product</u> development, enabling companies to gain that all-important <u>competitive</u> advantage. The 2011 *Innovation Awards for Industrial Design* recognize individuals with proven expertise in <u>research</u> and <u>development</u> who have come up with a design <u>concept</u> that responds to current market <u>trends</u> in the field of industrial design. The difference with this year's winner – he or she will have worked directly with the <u>consumer</u> as <u>co-creator</u> to come up with the winning concept.

7.1 screening criteria, market criteria, product criteria, financial criteria, must-have criteria, would-like criteria, key criteria

7.2 brainstorming – 3a, checklist – 2d, objective – 4b, subjective 1c

7.3 'We've been asked by a lot of people just how we grew so quickly, and the answer is actually really simple. A <u>consultation</u> process and <u>evaluation</u> of the <u>potential</u> market led to our original concept, which was to provide the best customer service possible. For example, we have a unique <u>distribution</u> policy that provides the benefit of free shipping both ways. Our customers will often buy ten pairs of shoes, select one pair they really like in the comfort of their own home and then return the other nine pairs to us.

We don't spend a lot of money on traditional means of <u>advertising</u> through <u>mass</u> media. Instead, we try to <u>differentiate</u> just our service and enhance the customer experience so that we get a lot of repeat customers, many of whom switch brands from our competitors. Much to our surprise, the <u>original</u> concept worked so well there was never any need to <u>modify</u> it. We produce shoes, there is nothing unique in the product <u>characteristics</u>, neither is our <u>portfolio</u> particularly extensive. However, what we did realise was that there were certain obvious commercial <u>realities</u>: everyone needs shoes, our prices are reasonable but still make a profit and, of course, we can do better than the competition!'

8.1 new product introduction, product champion, new-product project, product life-cycle, new product development process, product launch

Strategic planning	Concept generation	Pre-technical evaluation	Technical development	Commercialization	New product introduction
c Is there evidence of market size and technical feasibility to create a market opportunity?	d Is there market interest in the product concept, market viability, revenue potential, etc?	b Is it possible to deliver the new product technology?	a A tangible prototype is created and evaluated using both market and technical criteria.	f The product takes its ultimate form and marketing plans are evaluated.	e The product is finally put on the market.

8.3 1a, 2b, 3b, 4a, 5b, 6a

9.1

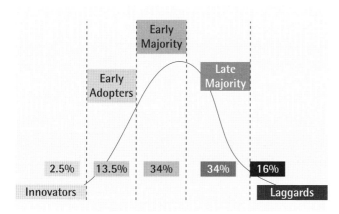

This curve shows the **diffusion** of an **innovation** in the market as it is **adopted** by groups of consumers over a period of time. It shows how very small groups of **innovators** are the first to try out new ideas, which are then **adopted** by other consumers. Some groups wait until the innovation is successful or until they need to own it. These are known as the **early majority** and **late majority**, respectively.

9.2 After appearing in a TV programme for would-be entrepreneurs, successful reggae singer, Levi Roots has developed a revolutionary business, selling Reggae Reggae Sauces, a range of hot spicy barbeque sauces and seasoning. Levi had a vision and soon secured investment in return for a substantial share of the equity in his company. Levi has gone on to win huge orders from major supermarket chains for his sauces, made to a secret forumula based on an original recipe from his grandmother in the Caribbean. Retailers now stock a growing range of flavours; pack sizes as well as a growing order book. This now highly successful business will soon be stocking a wide range of products. And there are hopes of substantial export sales in the near future.

9.3 Despite (2) enjoying huge success with the iPhone, (a) the latest object of desire, it seems that (4) even revolutionary designers, Apple (b) turn out innovation failures from time to time. Launched in 1996, the Bandai Pippin was Apple's effort to compete with the likes of Nintendo and Sony. Combining a networked computer with a home games console, Apple created the Pippin platform and hoped to license it to other companies. Bandai, looking for a way to get in to the games market, snapped it up. (1) Contributory factors leading (c) to such a spectacular failure included the fact that its library of games and software were poor in comparison with rival home consoles, and it was reputed that (3) only 42,000 Pippins were sold – (d) its projected break-even point barely met.

10.1 Copyrights protect material such as books, photographs, films, TV and music.

Patents protect new inventions and cover how inventions work; allow exclusive rights to manufacture, use or sell an invention.

Trademarks protect brand identities, symbols and logos that will distinguish an organization's products or services from those sold by another organization.

10.2 1 Patent attorney
2 To patent an idea or invention
3 Patent search
4 Patent application
5 Patent pending

10.3 We are not short of killer ideas or brainwaves. However, managers and senior staff have a significant role to play in seeking out opportunities for innovative ideas and in testing their feasibility. We can only survive and thrive if we all agree to work as follows:
- To protect the intellectual property rights of any ideas or innovations in the creative work that we do
- Where necessary, we need our partners and suppliers on individual projects to sign non-disclosure agreements before significant work is done
- To develop prototypes of new products
- To agree to have a full-scale patent search carried out
- To avoid any form of copyright violation that could damage the reputation of the company.

10.4 Wikipedia – the world's largest and most cited collaborative encyclopaedia is one example of content available under a creative commons licence. By allowing people to legally share content, this has since become one of the greatest cultural resources of the digital revolution.

Flickr – the photo sharing site grants copyright permissions to the creative work of photographers around the world, enabling millions of photos to be in 'the commons'.

11.1 customer focused, customer service, customer needs, customer wants, customer demand, customer requirements

11.2 1 supply of goods
2 production-led
3 sales-led
4 market-driven
5 high-pressure sales approach
6 apply marketing principles

11.3 1 Long-life battery, capacity to hold 200 titles, online retail facility (no use of polluting vehicles to deliver the books).
2 Tangible product, because the reader can buy the device and see the book on the screen.
3 Book shops (especially in railway stations and airports), department stores, large supermarkets, hi tech stores, on the Internet.
4 Speciality Kindles targeted according to age, gender, etc., Kindles offering different genres, etc.
5 Practical (no need for Wi-Fi hotspot or cables, etc.), size and weight, capacity, choice (500,000 books, magazines, etc.), payment options.

12.1 marketing planning, marketing management, marketing objectives, market development, market entry, market structure, market segment, market share, market trend, marketing strategies, market presence

12.2 a market segment, b market share, c market trend, d marketing objectives, e marketing strategies

12.3

Strengths	Weaknesses
b Coffee Independent is a brand built upon a <u>reputation</u> for outstanding customer service. g Coffee Independent has recently <u>expanded</u> its range of coffees and now includes fair trade products. j Despite the arrival of <u>copy-cat</u> brands onto the market recently, Coffee Independent has maintained its lead on the local market.	c Coffee Independent's recent attempts at establishing a market <u>presence</u> in France have not been entirely <u>profitable</u>. f In some regions of the UK the company does not have enough branches to ensure market <u>presence</u>.
Opportunities	**Threats**
a With its new fair-trade product lines the organization is set to update its mission statement to reflect its <u>ethical</u> values. d The company has earned respect amongst competitors for its ability to <u>exploit</u> opportunities for market development and <u>diversify</u> when necessary. k The results of a new gap <u>analysis</u> point to potential markets in the Middle East. However, this would involve significant resource <u>requirements</u> and a complete review of internal <u>performance</u>. i The company has been approached as a potential partner in a co-<u>branding</u> venture to sell products under the same brand name.	e Like some of its competitors, as Coffee Independent is a global <u>retailer</u>, it is likely to be <u>exposed</u> to political problems in countries where it has operations. h The company <u>depends</u> quite significantly <u>on</u> a relatively outdated IT system which threatens its ability to <u>compete</u> with the larger global <u>brands</u>.

13.1 distribute the product, tangible product, product life cycle, product awareness, be aware of the product, declining product

13.2 a intangible service, b retail outlets, c premises, d customer loyalty, e product life cycle

13.3 1 People

2 Process

3 Promotion

4 Price

5 Product

6 Place

7 Physical evidence

13.4 1e Research and development (R&D)

2c Introduction or launch

3b Growth

4a Maturity

5d Saturation – to decline

14.1

S	T	E	E	P
b, g	j	d	a, c, h, k	f, i, e

14.2 marketing instrument, management instrument, strategic instrument
Synonyms: tool for carrying out an activity, document

14.3 'I'm a bit of a health freak and as I knew the producers of the local spring water were trying to <u>establish</u> the market in the region, I proposed my services free of charge. The marketing manager determined a <u>suitable</u> sample and my <u>research</u> brief for the <u>assignment</u> was to survey the consumption pattern for the 20–25 age group, the <u>findings</u> of which would then be put to a <u>consumer</u> panel for further analysis. The data <u>collection</u> stage was fun but I did spend a lot of time designing the <u>questionnaire</u> so that it could be used both face to face in <u>semi-structured</u> interviews as well as via an online resource. I know the <u>competitive</u> position of this particular producer is currently fairly poor, but I hope that on <u>analysis</u> of the data I was able to collect they will see the potential at least for this particular age group of <u>likely</u> customers.'

15.1

go		
		communities
	online	questionnaire
basic		services
		environment

15.2 SMM will design you a <u>blog</u> to enable you to reach clients from your particular <u>niche</u> market as well as access the relevant <u>communities</u> of practice through existing social <u>networking</u> sites. SMM can also help boost awareness of your website, by ensuring search engine <u>optimization</u>. Give potential customers up-to-the-minute information on your product line. Have existing clients post testimonials and participate in online <u>questionnaires</u>. An informal non-sales approach allowing you to interact directly with your customers and gain valuable insight into their needs and wants.

If technology is an issue, then SMM has the know-how. Get potential customers excited about your latest service by sending them <u>podcasts</u> of interviews with those who have already tried and tested it. Or if it's <u>digital</u> downloads you offer, then send them a <u>downloadable</u> sample. SMM has the technical means, so sit back and relax.

SMM will also give you that all-important advice on how to exploit the potential of your website: how to attract content-related <u>advertisers</u>; how to ensure '<u>stickiness</u>' so that visitors to your website hang around a little longer; how much to charge for <u>subscription</u> services; and how to decide which services to charge a <u>premium</u> for.

16.1

buzz   marketing
clicks and mortar   site
community   feature
discussion   forum
fully   online
interactive   feature
online   business
online   retailer
physical   outlet
product   champions
target   audience
traditional   advertising media
viral   marketing

16.2 Voted the fashion industry's <u>online retailer</u> of the year in 2009, SOX.com started out life as a <u>physical outlet</u>: a small stall in the trendy Spitalfields Market in London. Taking it slowly, SOX.com then became a so-called <u>clicks and mortar</u> site, eventually going <u>fully online</u> in 2005. Unlike other <u>online businesses</u> in the fashion world, it has witnessed phenomenal success, and now stocks over 32,000 styles, with a product range aimed primarily at the 16 to 34 age group, but which in reality appeals to a much wider public. Our use of technology goes beyond <u>traditional advertising media</u>; one of our more <u>interactive features</u> is our online 'catwalk', a unique tool enabling *fashionistas* to see our products on moving models. Ours is a relatively young <u>target audience</u>, so it's very easy to promote sales through <u>viral marketing</u> – via Facebook, for example. SOX.com also engages in <u>buzz marketing</u> to help sell our new lines. We encourage our <u>product champions</u> to participate in <u>discussion forums</u> – where they discuss the latest styles available in our online store. Indeed this <u>community feature</u> was only added fairly recently but has proved highly successful …

16.3 1c, 2a, 3d, 4b

17.1 1c, 2a, 3g, 4b, 5e, 6d, 7f

17.2

Noun phrase	Verb phrase	Adjectival phrase
global risks	prioritize risks	risk aware
risk profile	assess risk	
risk management process	deal with risk	
potential risk		
risk and continuity management		
risk management policy		

17.3 3 As part of the <u>operations management</u> team, I chair a working group to evaluate and monitor both our current and our planned projects to identify the nature of the risks, the probability of occurrence and the consequences. From this we produce a <u>risk profile</u> so that we can see where the company might be <u>vulnerable</u> and then <u>prioritize/assess</u> the identified risks.

4 We identify <u>global</u> risks as well as issues that could affect us on a more local scale, such as the risk to our <u>supply</u> chain, as we rely a lot on <u>outsourcing</u> and we also <u>subcontract</u> processes to external suppliers.

1 From this analysis, we have established an effective risk <u>management process</u> across the organization by:
 • systematically identifying, evaluating and prioritizing <u>potential</u> risks. For this we have a written risk <u>management policy</u> that sets out responsibilities of key staff.
 • developing an organizational culture in which individuals are risk <u>aware</u> but are not afraid of taking decisions and undertaking activities which involve acceptable levels of risk.

2 We regularly collect data and evaluate information from every project to monitor further risks and review the <u>contingency</u> plans which have been put in place. We also monitor and review the effectiveness of the risk <u>management process</u> in the company, identifying potential improvements and making changes where necessary.

5 We then pass all this information on to our <u>emergency planning</u> officers and <u>business continuity</u> managers, who ensure continuity of service to our key customers and the protection of our reputation following a disruptive event.

18.1 Q: Hanna.com was named European Online Retailer of the Year in 2011 and I understand your website is currently attracting over five million visitors a month. With so much interest, how do you deal with <u>supply chain management</u>?

A: Our <u>supply chain</u> is run on a fairly traditional basis. In fact we <u>hold stock</u> of over 20,000 product styles in our warehouse. We don't expect the supplier to <u>bear the extra cost</u> of storing the products for us.

Q: I understand that some of your <u>subcontractors</u> were accused a few years ago of unethical conduct?

A: Unfortunately, yes. We carried out <u>supplier audits</u> in several countries and these careful checks revealed that some <u>suppliers</u> had been hiring underage employees. We immediately took <u>remedial steps</u> and we've increased the number of factories <u>audited</u> each year from 29 to 106.

Q: Have you considered creating a <u>formal alliance</u> with some of your suppliers so that you work together with their management to avoid similar occurrences?

A: We feel that owning shares in our suppliers is a more effective way to exert control, rather than entering a formal partnership. So having <u>an equity stake in</u> our subcontractors' companies may well be the way forward.

18.2 approved suppliers, initial order, trade directory, procurement department, repeat purchases, value analysis

1 Procurement department
2 Value analysis
3 Trade directory
4 Approved suppliers

18.3 As the public sector faces efficiency drives and budget cuts resulting from the credit crunch, Sue Rippin, business development manager at Northgate Arinso, an HR <u>outsourcing</u> company, expects to see a growth in business. She highlighted councils as prime areas for growth in <u>outsourced processes</u>, because their <u>core competences</u> remain relatively limited. They are specialists in supplying services such as Health and Education, rather than <u>non-core processes</u> such as <u>payroll</u> management. Rippin added that 'outsourcing is very competitive. As <u>vendors</u>, offering our services, we are selected using a rigorous <u>rating system</u> and have agreed to a <u>legally binding</u> contract. The standard of our performance will be <u>monitored</u> to ensure that we keep to the agreed contract; otherwise we could face legal action'.

19.1 1 benchmarks, 2 customer's specification, 3 fit for purpose, 4 internal supply chain, 5 quality assurance, 6 'the customer rules'

19.2 Q: The effective management of water resources and access to clean drinking water are major concerns for governments. What is the role of the ISO in this process?

A: It is important to understand that the role of the ISO is not prescriptive; the organization merely provides the guidelines for a <u>quality management system</u>.

Q: What does standardizing service provision worldwide involve?

A: The aim of the ISO is to work with regional and national authorities to determine the level of results to be achieved and then to establish the means by which their procedures are <u>implemented</u>. As with the private sector, these authorities will be required to <u>document procedures</u> and demonstrate that they are <u>complying fully with</u> the ISO guidelines. Just as in the case of the private sector, they may carry out an <u>internal audit</u>, that is, an objective internal appraisal of the organization's procedures and performance to ensure compliance.

19.3 The Eskisehir Maternity and Child Illness Hospital seeks to provide patients with a level of care that exceeds expectations, with nurses in particular being encouraged to <u>build partnerships</u> directly with their patients, adding value to their experiences through new ways of providing care. By promoting the free circulation of ideas and personal growth the Eskisehir also strives to <u>empower</u> its staff. Indeed this is a hospital that has developed an environment of trust and responsibility, actively <u>nurturing</u> creativity and innovation from its employees. This means there is a positive mindset <u>embedded</u> within the professional environment, which helps to retain its staff and ensure a <u>sustainable</u> future for the hospital. As well as focusing on the human factor, the hospital employs a sound basis of <u>fact-based</u> decision making. The organization has achieved a <u>balanced set of results</u>, in terms of patient and staff satisfaction as well as economic efficiency. In fact, its performance has demonstrated an ability to act as a <u>role-model</u> hospital within the region. The panel felt the Eskisehir had achieved a certain level of <u>sustainable excellence</u> that merited this year's award.

20.1 1b, 2d, 3a, 4c, 5e

20.2

Loyal to the brand	When an individual always buys the product of a particular company rather than similar products offered by other companies
Recruiting customers	Persuading customers to start buying your company's products
Retaining existing customers	Making sure that customers continue to purchase your product or service
Customer relationship management	Systematic policies to monitor and ensure customer satisfaction

20.3 The appointment of our new Chief Executive with a marketing background acted as an important catalyst in bringing about <u>culture</u> change and <u>shaping policies</u> to make Eurostar more customer orientated.

He suggested we bring our <u>customers' stories</u> to life by using <u>customer journey mapping</u>. This was carried out using a heart monitor, <u>tracking</u> the highs and lows of the journey – the <u>contact points</u> where they interacted with <u>customer-facing</u> staff or machines, the times when people became bored or even experienced fear, for example, when entering the tunnel. By making the journey themselves, staff were able to get <u>close</u> to their <u>customers</u>.

After experiencing the service from the <u>customer's perspective</u>, staff suggested really practical solutions to problems, which not only improved the experience but, in many cases, reduced costs too.

21.1 1 stock control, 2 inventory management system, 3 state-of-the-art, 4 inventory, 5 reorder level 6 margin of safety, 7 buffer stock, 8 just in time, 9 discounts, 10 economies of scale

21.2 online tendering, tender documents, pre-tender queries, to evaluate a tender, to put out to tender, put in a tender

Tenderers = people who tender (offer) their goods or services

A tender is a formal written offer to do work or supply goods or services for an agreed price and under agreed conditions.

21.3 Richard Maybey, a manager in a major European financial services group, was asked about his experience of using online <u>procurement</u> services.

'I am responsible for an annual procurement <u>budget</u> of 20m euros. Major areas in which I have to <u>source</u> goods and services include IT equipment and catering and cleaning services.

In recent years we have moved to a robust system to <u>put</u> our requirements <u>out</u> to <u>tender</u>. I simply upload the <u>tender documents</u> with our particular <u>specifications</u> to our website and wait for the suppliers to contact me and the time taken to find <u>prospective suppliers</u> is significantly reduced. The process is a <u>secure</u> online system and even uses a code to <u>encrypt</u> the private details the suppliers provide about their business to ensure confidentiality.

We have also used commercial online tendering services. The only problem I find with services targeting the financial sector is that the sites are not always <u>user-friendly</u> and lack <u>guidance</u> notes to take you through the features of the site. And if you have any <u>pre-tender</u> <u>queries</u>, the information in the <u>FAQs</u> page is often insufficient. However, there is sometimes a <u>discussion forum</u>, where you can actually talk about issues with other people in the same line of work. There is often a section where people compare their experiences, good or bad, of particular suppliers, which can be useful, but this is only for <u>registered users</u> so you need a <u>subscription</u> first. The cost of this payment can be quite high.'

22.1 Resources requirement: our <u>human resources</u> strategy, that is, identifying why we are recruiting and how to match the people we employ and the jobs they do to our company's goals, is an important element of our annual planning.

Person requirements: we draw up a job <u>description</u> profiling <u>competencies</u>, that is the skills and the knowledge required to do the job as well as the essential attitudes or characteristics to fit into the organization.

Job <u>advertisement</u>: this is usually done online.

Screening the applicants: completed application <u>forms</u> are <u>sifted</u> to ensure that we only interview suitable candidates. Apart from interviews, we also use <u>assessment</u> centres where we carry out <u>competency</u> profiling.

Invitation to interview: we then ask the <u>applicants</u> selected from the screening process (the shortlisted candidates) to attend a selection <u>panel</u> in which a group of interviewers explore the skills, qualifications and knowledge they can bring to the job.

Appointment: after the interviews have been completed we make a <u>conditional</u> offer and contact the <u>referees</u> once the successful candidate has accepted the terms and conditions of their <u>contract</u> of <u>employment</u>. They then have to work out their <u>notice</u> period, that is the length of time they have to continue working for their present employer after they officially resign from that job.

<u>Induction</u> programme: every new member of the team spends a day with the team with whom they will be working. They are introduced to the working procedure and different team roles.

22.2 equal treatment, equal access, equal opportunities, equality

22.3 QualityTime plc has <u>an equal access</u> policy. That means we welcome applications from all sections of the community, regardless of race, religion, disability or other differences. In fact, we believe that this <u>diversity</u> in our <u>workforce</u> is a strength of our organization.

We also believe that <u>discrimination</u> against any group of workers has no place in a modern company. We comply with <u>current legislation</u> under UK and EU law, and under our <u>employment</u> policies, <u>equal treatment</u> is guaranteed for all members of staff, including those on <u>temporary</u> contracts or part-time workers as well as full-time employees.

23.1 job rotation (1), job enlargement (2), job security (3), job satisfaction (4), job enrichment (5)

23.2 1d, 2a, 3c, 4e, 5b

23.3 Working for the UN, I feel a certain sense of <u>engagement</u>, with the work itself, because it is contributing to the greater good. Also I have good <u>interpersonal</u> relationships with my <u>colleagues</u> who work beside me in the team because it is a really <u>collaborative</u> work environment. However, international organizations have a reputation for top-heavy administrative procedures and <u>red</u> tape, you know, too many unimportant rules often resulting in too much <u>micro</u> management.

Sadly for secretaries there is little in terms of career <u>advancement</u> and <u>personal</u> development and <u>salary</u> levels are low. Most of my <u>peers</u>, that is, the other secretaries who work at the same level as me, are multilingual, and we frequently act as unofficial interpreters, as well as taking <u>charge</u> of extremely sensitive UN documents. However, while working <u>conditions</u> are generally good and the employee's <u>well-being</u> is taken into consideration, <u>motivation</u> remains low. There is little <u>recognition</u> of our achievements, a critical factor in terms of overall job <u>satisfaction</u>.'

24.1

	Advantages of 360-degree feedback	Disadvantages of 360-degree feedback
Combined opinion gives a more accurate and objective view.	✓	
Comments are difficult to ignore when expressed by a number of colleagues.	✓	
It can be motivating for people who undervalue themselves.	✓	
It can generate an environment of suspicion, unless managed openly and honestly.		✓
Some skills, such as leadership, are best judged by subordinates and peers rather than superiors.	✓	

24.2 Coaching, mentoring, buddy systems, induction training, shadowing

24.3 'This afternoon we're going to talk about our <u>performance appraisal</u> system, which if done effectively, i.e. carried out in a <u>non-threatening environment</u>, can actually contribute to your sense of <u>employee empowerment</u>. Our company has a <u>flattened hierarchy</u>, so we prefer to use <u>360-degree appraisal</u> as opposed to the traditional top down <u>appraisal</u>. The <u>appraisers</u> include those from your own level as well as those above and below you. First you carry out a <u>self-assessment</u>. Then we ask your <u>peers</u> and your <u>line manager</u> to give their opinion. These appraisals, usually done through <u>online appraisal systems</u>, are sent to a <u>facilitator</u> who will ensure the feedback you receive is entirely <u>confidential</u>. <u>Team appraisals</u> are also carried out, even for <u>virtual teams</u>. And you'll be pleased to hear the branch managers do not escape. They are subjected to an evaluation from their subordinates known as <u>upward feedback</u>.'

25.1
1 Forming – The early encounters between the individual members, when people do not yet know the others well.
2 Storming – Individuals test their strengths and approaches to the task facing the group; disagreements and conflict may arise and have to be resolved.
3 Norming – Group members work productively together.
4 Performing – The group becomes more cohesive, with clearly established roles and working procedures.
5 Adjourning – The group dissolves as the project ends.

25.2
1 to get down to
2 to get on with something
3 to get through
4 to get on with someone
5 to get to know each other

25.3

Motivation	Passion to work for reasons beyond money or status. Drive to achieve
Self-regulation	Ability to control or redirect disruptive impulses and think before acting
Social skills	Proficiency in managing relationships and building effectiveness in leading change
Empathy	Ability to understand and respond to the emotions and reactions of other people
Self-awareness	Ability to recognize and understand your moods, emotions and drives, as well as their effect on others

25.4

Samira: The <u>initial</u> <u>exchange</u>, when you open the conversation with a potential management candidate is very revealing, I find. If they can't establish good <u>interpersonal</u> relationships quickly, they are not likely to get on with their team and cope with the different <u>personality types</u> within any one team.

Carmel: The ones that <u>perform</u> <u>poorly</u> lack flexibility in their dealings with others. We need someone who can engage well in <u>teamwork</u> and develop enthusiasm and <u>team spirit</u> to <u>build</u> a <u>winning</u> team.

Samira: Yes, that type of leader encourages <u>collaboration</u> and a spirit of <u>camaraderie</u> and friendship in the team.

Carmel: Oh, yes, they need <u>emotional</u> <u>intelligence</u> as well as demonstrating a certain degree of <u>determination</u> and 'toughness' for effective leadership.

26.1 sources of knowledge, collect knowledge, share knowledge, knowledge management, acquire knowledge, develop knowledge, knowledge networking, explicit knowledge, tacit knowledge

26.2 continuous learning – 2a, double-loop learning – 6b, learning environment – 3e, learning organization – 4c, learning process – 1f, no-blame culture – 5d

26.3 With almost one-third of companies now operating a formal talent strategy, anyone with any interest in HR management will be aware of the significance of this concept in terms of organizational <u>best</u> <u>practice</u>. Organizations have recognized the need for continuous investment in the <u>intellectual</u> <u>capital</u> of their staff to generate competitive advantage. This has placed increased pressure on HR to demonstrate their <u>added</u> <u>value</u> and justify investments as 'business critical'.

Following the recent recession, many organizations have revived their attempts to <u>retain</u> and attract the <u>high flyers</u>, by putting <u>talent</u> <u>management</u> firmly back onto the executive agenda. Investing in the right people and <u>stretching</u> their capabilities is once more a key focus for HR.

Programmes originally focused on the top talent but then came the recognition that everyone needs to realize their full potential; the result of this has been a blended approach to talent management and monitoring. Many organizations focus on managing selected subgroups, such as graduate populations and those with <u>research expertise</u>.

Based on research carried out by the Chartered Institute of Personnel and Development, this paper demonstrates recent trends in the development of talent <u>management</u>.

27.1 1c, 2d, 3e, 4a, 5b

27.2 <u>Active</u> management-by-exception: they focus attention on mistakes and deviations from what is expected of me.

<u>Passive</u> management-by-exception: problems have to be critical before the person I am rating will take action.

Non-leadership <u>Laissez-faire</u>: my manager avoids getting involved when important issues arise.

<u>Transformational</u> leadership

Inspirational motivation: in my mind this person is a symbol of success and accomplishment.

<u>Intellectual stimulation</u>: they introduce new projects and new challenges.

<u>Individual consideration</u>: they listen to my concerns.

<u>Idealized influence</u>: I am ready to trust the person to overcome any obstacle.

27.3 From the case study it is evident that the explorer Ernest Shackleton demonstrated many of the <u>personality traits</u> identified by Warren Bennis in his research. Like any explorer, Shackleton could definitely be described as a <u>risk taker</u> but he also had a <u>clear vision</u> which he put into action through his management skills, making sure the appropriate equipment and <u>resources</u> were in place before the expedition began. He also made sure he had a <u>well-balanced team</u>, and showed an active management approach in carrying out <u>team-building activities</u> to <u>create bonds</u> between the team and make sure that they worked cooperatively together. However, his achievement was not simply about reaching the Antarctic; his <u>charismatic leadership</u> when his ship was trapped in the ice showed his ability to <u>deal with adversity</u> and ensured the survival of his team. He also earned the trust and respect of his team by his <u>integrity</u> in setting a personal example of hard work and in his <u>fairness</u> and communication skills when <u>managing conflicts</u> that arose.

28.1 cross-cultural competences, cross-cultural differences, corporate culture, cultural assumptions, cultural awareness, cultural differences, cultural diversity, cultural impact, cultural stereotypes, culture shock, prevailing culture

The Quest Cultural Training course will provide you with:
- A better understanding of the cultural <u>impact</u> of your business and <u>corporate</u> culture in countries where you operate
- The opportunity to enhance your cultural <u>awareness</u> and develop cross-cultural <u>competences</u> by giving you practical tools to reduce cross-cultural misunderstanding
- The opportunity to examine your own cultural <u>assumptions</u> and avoid seeing others through narrow cultural <u>stereotypes</u>.

28.2

Small power distance – New Zealand	Large power distance – Malaysia
More individualist – the UK	More collectivist – China
Strong uncertainty avoidance – Japan	Weak uncertainty avoidance – the UK
More masculine values – the USA	More feminine values – the Netherlands

28.3 1 values, 2 codes of behaviour/norm/unwritten rules, 3 comfort zone, 4 'silo' mentality (This is a metaphor based on farming, where food is stored for a long time in containers called silos, and is therefore not available for consumption.)

29.1 Fixed assets, current assets, current liabilities, long-term assets

29.2 cost control, direct cost, indirect costs, fixed costs, variable costs, allocate costs, cost centre, real cost, activity-based costing

29.3 1f, 2h, 3g, 4a, 5c, 6b, 7d, 8e

30.1 An international hotel chain decides to purchase four hotels, including one located in a prime UK tourist spot, which it believes would provide generous return on assets. The vendor sells the hotels as a going concern. Making a business valuation was not a simple task. Not only had the cost of its assets been noted at their book value, less depreciation, but also the vendors were not taking into account the time value of money. The concept of fair value was used to arrive at a final, more realistic price that was slightly higher than market value. This is a market comparables approach. Another approach they could have considered uses the projected free cash flow/FCF, and applies a time-related discount rate to estimate the net present value/NPV.

30.2
Susie: Look at Easiphone – its gross profit margin is really high, but its current ratio is low.
Kaoru: Is that the same as the working capital ratio?
Susie: Yes. Look, it has liabilities of £80 milllion but its assets are only £50 million. It would have a problem with short-term liquidity.
Kaoru: I agree. It might not be able to pay its debts.
Susie: So its profitability isn't as good as it looks. Did you check the solvency ratio?
Kaoru: Yes, if you take off tax and depreciation, that ratio is only 16% – it doesn't look as though Easiphone will be able to survive in the long term.
Susie: So far we think Easiphone is not likely to give shareholders a good return on investment. What about Youtalk?
Kaoru: Well, I think there is a better ROC, that's the return on the capital that has been invested in the business.
Susie: And the investors think it's pretty healthy, too: I checked out the Price/Earnings (P/E) ratio on Youtalk and if you divide the share price by earnings from the year 2010, the market value of the shares has really gone up.
Kaoru: So, those investors must think their earnings are going to increase in the future. I suppose Youtalk would be the best one to invest in.

31.1 credit rating, credit score, credit search, creditworthiness, credit history, credit transfer, credit bureau(x)

31.2 Becoming an Alfa borrower
1 *What kind of credit search does Alfa Finance carry out?*
   When making a loan application you will be giving permission for our credit bureau to access your credit records to determine your creditworthiness.
2 *If I have a bad credit rating, can I borrow from Alfa Finance?*
   We regret that those with a history of bad debt will have their applications turned down. (note: bad debt (noun phrase) bad-debt (adjective form)
3 *What does the APR cover?*
   It covers the annual interest you pay to the depositor, i.e. the person lending money, and our fee. As a 'social marketplace' the interest rates are set by our lenders.
4 *Is it possible to settle my loan early?*
   No problem. Alfa allows you to repay your loan before it reaches maturity by using electronic transfer, or direct debit. Just click on 'Settle in Full'.

5 *What happens if I <u>default</u> on my payments?*
We may reassess your **schedule** to create a more <u>customized</u> solution, suitable for your personal needs.

Becoming an Alpha lender:

6 *If I want to make my money available to others, what are the lending <u>criteria</u>?*
Simple, you must be 18 years old, an Australian resident, with an Australian bank account.

7 *Does Alfa Finance protect my money against <u>fraud</u>?*
Certainly, and money against <u>laundering</u>, to prevent criminals hiding their money through our accounts. Alfa employs safety measures similar to those of banks.

31.3 1c, 2e, 3a, 4b, 5d

32.1 1b, 2f, 3d, 4a, 5i, 6g, 7h, 8c, 9e

32.2 Investor Warren Buffett yesterday purchased $300m worth of <u>debt</u> <u>offering</u> from the struggling motorcycle manufacturer, Harley-Davidson. The <u>venture</u> capitalist, who already owns <u>stocks</u> in US giants General Electric and Mars, is seeking to capitalize on the current economic crisis. Along with other <u>noteholders</u>, Buffet will receive 15% interest on the debt <u>securities</u>. Although this high interest rate will cut earnings to 18 cents a share, the <u>stock</u> market reacted positively to this show of confidence from the famous business <u>angel</u> and Harley's shares rose by over 15%.

33.1 mergers and acquisitions, market-extension mergers, product-extension mergers, cross-border mergers and acquisitions, merger waves, vertical integration, horizontal integration, post-merger integration

33.2 1 horizontal integration, 2 market-extension merger, 3 vertical integration, 4 Joint venture, or strategic alliance, 5 Conglomeration.

33.3 Once the target company has been identified it is important that an executive is put in place to take responsibility for the process up to the <u>post-merger</u> integration stage. As well as overseeing that operations are re-<u>structured</u> and the new company re-<u>branded</u>, where necessary, such a manager needs to ensure due <u>diligence</u> is practised and that the newly formed company complies with the <u>anti-trust</u> laws of the country to avoid any <u>anti-competitive</u> practices. A successful integration manager would employ a <u>transformational</u> approach, to create true <u>synergy</u>, making sure the 'return on <u>talent</u>' was guaranteed by encouraging and rewarding key workers so that the new company would not lose their knowledge and experience.

34.1 1 a sole proprietor
2 a private limited company
3 an unqualified opinion
4 a legal entity
5 a public limited company (plc)
6 a qualified opinion

34.2 According to the UK <u>code</u> of <u>corporate</u> <u>governance</u>, shareholders have the role of appointing the <u>board</u> of <u>directors</u>. These directors are <u>fiduciaries</u>, that is agents on behalf of the shareholders, with <u>collective</u> responsibility for the success of the company and <u>accountability</u> for its failures. In other words, they must demonstrate good <u>stewardship</u>, taking care of the company for which they are responsible and always showing openness, or <u>transparency</u>, towards their <u>principals</u>, the shareholders. The board should include <u>non-executive</u> directors, responsible for ensuring that objectives are reached. Supervising the effectiveness of the board is the <u>chairman</u>. The <u>division</u> of responsibilities between the chairman and CEO should be clear to avoid any potential <u>conflict</u> of interest, given the amount of <u>inside</u> information to which they have access.

Election of the board is carried out during the <u>Annual General Meeting</u>, which serves as a forum for shareholders to elect or remove the chairman, question the board's decisions, raise issues of the fairness of executive <u>compensation</u>, where necessary, and appoint the <u>external auditors</u>, accountants from a specialist accounting company who check the company's balance sheet.

Serving on a board involves some amount of <u>remuneration</u>, which can take the form of <u>incentives</u> to stimulate performance, such as <u>bonuses</u>, extra payments directly related to performance, or <u>share options</u> which link <u>executives</u>' wealth to that of the company. In all their activities, the directors and shareholders are responsible for conforming to the national laws such as the <u>Companies Act</u> (UK) and its equivalents worldwide, such as the US anti-trust laws.

35.1 'A Heat Map is a simple tool prepared by the <u>treasury</u> department to demonstrate not only the <u>exposure</u> to possible risks for each business unit but also overall corporate earnings that are at risk. It uses colour to show areas of high risk, with red showing the more <u>volatile</u> areas, accounting for 10% of the company's capital at risk, in this example. From this a risk profile is drawn up and the board of directors devises an appropriate <u>risk-management</u> strategy. Where the company has an investment <u>portfolio</u>, there may be a need for <u>diversification</u> to <u>spread</u> the risk. Risks can also be <u>mitigated</u> by <u>hedging</u>, for example, holding a currency <u>reserve</u>, in case there are changes in the <u>exchange</u> rate. Companies <u>regulated</u> by the government are not always free to act as they wish, but must factor in the costs of fulfilling the terms of their <u>operating licence</u>. Companies also have to weigh up not only the <u>tangible</u> benefits of certain risk management strategies, such as capital <u>efficiency</u>, but also the <u>intangible benefits</u>: for example, investment in safety measures in car design might be expensive, but enhances <u>brand reputation</u>.'

35.2 1 investment vehicle, 2 mutual fund, 3 Islamic banking, 4 ethical investment, 5 hedge fund

36.1

Type of investment products and lending	derivatives, mortgages, sub-prime debt, interbank lending, The London Interbank Overnight Rate (LIBOR)
Institutions and markets involved	Central banks, Federal Reserve, Wall Street, capital markets
Things that went wrong	bad debts, bank run, bankrupt, meltdown, recession, sovereign debt crisis, toxic assets, credit crunch
Ways of tackling the crisis and making banks safe	checks and balances, equity buffers, underwrite, waive competition law, bank capitalization, quantitative easing, regulation

36.2

Casey: So, did you understand what really caused the credit crunch? I'm not sure that I did.

Ashraf: Well, I get the impression it was <u>leverage</u> that caused the problem.

Casey: You mean people were using borrowed money to borrow more money?

Ashraf: Yes. So as well as the real banks with all their elaborate systems of <u>checks and balances</u> that they use to avoid risky lending, there was also a whole <u>shadow banking system</u> of other companies lending and <u>securitizing</u> risky products.

Casey: So what you mean is they were turning these things like <u>sub-prime</u> mortgages into securities to sell on the markets?

Ashraf: Exactly, and the banks were buying them up. The problem with <u>leverage</u> is that the loss is greater to the investor when things start to go wrong; in reality they are unable to sustain the debt. However, as the banks were <u>too big to fail</u>, governments had to bail them out and buy up their debts.

Casey: The lecturer called that <u>underwriting</u>, I think?

Ashraf: Yes. And of course some governments like Greece and Iceland couldn't pay their debts, so that's when the <u>sovereign debt crisis</u> came about.

Casey: Oh, OK, I think I've a better understanding of it all. Thanks, Ashraf.

37.1 aggressive marketing, bargaining power, competitive position, core competencies, existing market, generic strategies, market leader, niche market, potential entrants, substitute products

37.2 Let's consider the <u>competitive position</u> of companies within the global automobile industry. While suppliers of auto parts are plentiful, they are not considered a threat in terms of profit. In fact, from a <u>strategic marketing</u> point of view, some of their products could be regarded as

<u>complementors</u> to be marketed alongside the cars. However, other suppliers of inputs to the car industry, such as organized labour, can be a powerful force. Buyers (auto dealerships, car rental firms and individual consumers) remain unorganized but can negotiate on price. Competition amongst <u>existing</u> car firms further strengthens the customer's <u>bargaining power</u>. Successful <u>market penetration</u> is costly, which means there is little threat from <u>new entrants</u> to the market. There is little cause for concern with regard to <u>substitute products</u>, as despite alternatives – motorbikes, bicycles, public transport – most people prefer to purchase their own car. So there is unlikely to be a <u>shift in consumer demand</u> in the foreseeable future. However, <u>rivalry</u> within the industry itself is particularly intense, resulting in highly <u>aggressive marketing</u> campaigns. There is a <u>high volume of sales</u> but oversupply occurs due to enlarged production capacity, while <u>differentiation</u> proves difficult, except in <u>niche markets</u>, such as sports cars: <u>diversification</u> into new markets has fairly limited potential. As a result of such <u>competitive forces,</u> the auto industry bears only moderate profits.

37.3 (Sample answers)

Force	Strength of force	Comment and trends
Buyers	Moderate to strong	Customers have low switching costs as they change cars every few years and can choose a different model each time. They will choose the manufacturer with the most competitive deal.
Suppliers	Moderate	Most auto inputs are commodity products so their manufacturers are highly dependent on the car firms. However, labour can be a powerful force for some firms (e.g. General Motors and the French auto firms).
Substitute products	Low	For those living in towns and cities, it is public transport. Motorbikes and bicycles have limited sales.
Potential entrants	Low	Economies of scale make it very difficult to produce cars profitably without major investments in capital, labour and distribution. New technologies in drive and power systems are being introduced primarily by the automakers themselves.
Rivalry	High	Because of high capital costs and worldwide overcapacity, firms compete fiercely for new (and each other's) customers. Aggressive marketing campaigns seek to increase the competition.

38.1

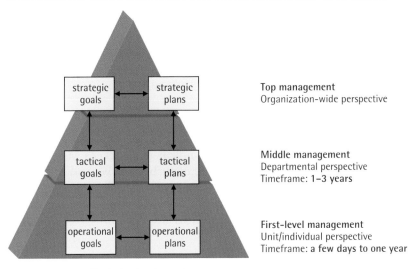

Strategic planning cycle

38.2 1 core values, 2 scenario planning, 3 value creation, 4 situational analysis, 5 strategy investment, 6 contingency plan, 7 multi-market activities, 8 corporate strategy

38.3 (Sample answer)

Amazon's core values are to develop a company that puts the customer completely at the centre of its activities. Critical factors for the company's success are ensuring a high-quality service as well as price control – this will satisfy both supplier and distributor.

39.1 1d, 2b, 3e, 4c, 5f, 6a

39.2 Faced with <u>pressure</u> for change, in the form of serious overseas competition, Xerox set a goal of reducing manufacturing costs at its New York copier plant through outsourcing certain electrical components, thus eliminating 150 jobs. The <u>key players</u> in the situation were the workforce. It might be expected that they would be <u>opponents</u> of change as they had a <u>vested interest</u> in maintaining the <u>status quo</u> to keep their jobs. However, the company had a history of good relations with their workforce, so union leaders and managers became <u>allies</u>, working together to overcome the <u>opposition/resistance</u> to change.

The diagram on the opposite page shows the major <u>driving</u> and <u>restraining</u> forces. Union leaders and management studied ways to save money, which finally led to eliminating certain healthcare benefits. In return, the company promised no layoffs for three years. By reducing these <u>restraining</u> forces, changes were agreed on which reduced cost levels without eliminating jobs. This case study illustrates how <u>force field</u> analysis can be applied as a <u>management tool</u> to help employees <u>come to terms</u> with change.

39.3 (sample answers)

1 The IT workers demonstrated active resistance to the introduction of PAN by voicing their opinions about the suitability of the product.

2 The presentation acted as a catalyst that encouraged the employees to accept the new package.

3 The IT employees were co-opted as opposed to coerced, or forced; resisters were given the chance to become involved in the proposed change and leave their comfort zone of the previous familiar system. Being involved in the decision strengthened their commitment. They finally came to terms with the decision to implement a new application.

40.1 (Sample answer)

S – The project required a specific objective of building a tunnel of required length.

M – The result was a dramatic reduction in traffic congestion and diversion of floodwater away from the district.

A – The Icelandic construction firm worked with local specialists to come to an agreement regarding the best way to resolve excavation issues.

R – It would have been unrealistic not to consider working with local experts, without whose specialized knowledge the project might not have succeeded.

T – The time set was sufficient for the project to be completed on time.

40.2 Initially, in order to achieve our <u>vision</u> statement we tried to implement Drucker's <u>MBO process</u> by setting <u>participative</u> goals and rewarding employee contribution. We had hoped that these objectives would <u>trickle</u> <u>down</u> to those dealing directly with the callers. However, we soon realized that the goal of finishing calls within seven minutes was not being met; calls were becoming more complex or there was a faulty new product, and operators were finishing calls early to meet targets, leaving customers frustrated. So we considered a contingency mechanism. We gave call types priority rankings depending on the problem presented by the caller. We also reassessed resource allocation and took on more staff to handle the calls. By monitoring progress, we had picked up the shift in the goal environment and goals were changed accordingly. We also built in accountability checkpoints, where the staff could decide for themselves if the caller's needs had been met or refer them to a supervisor. This empowered staff and helped them to feel accountable for their decisions. We learned that you can't just cascade decisions downwards, you need participation and empowerment: after all, that is the overarching premise of MBO.

40.3 1 decision-making software, **2** algorithm, **3** acronym, **4** organizational politics

Index

competitive business
/kəmˈpetətɪv ˈbɪznəs/ 4
competitive environment
/kəmˈpetətɪv ɪnˈvaɪərənmənt/ 38
competitive position
/kəmˈpetətɪv pəˈzɪʃn/ 14, 37
competitor /kəmˈpetɪtə/ 12
complementors /ˌkɒmpləˈmentəz/ 37
complex hierarchies
/ˈkɒmpleks ˈhaɪərɑːkiz/ 2
comply fully with
/kəmˈplaɪ ˈfʊli wɪð/ 19
comply with current legislation
/kəmˈplaɪ wɪð ˈkʌrənt ˌledʒɪsˈleɪʃn/ 22
computer-aided design
/kəmˈpjuːtə ˈeɪdɪd dɪˈzaɪn/ 9
concept generation
/ˈkɒnsept ˌdʒenəˈreɪʃn/ 8
conditional offer /kənˈdɪʃnəl ˈɒfə/ 22
configuration /kənˌfɪɡəˈreɪʃn/ 38
conflict of interest
/ˈkɒnflɪkt əv ˈɪntrəst/ 34
conglomeration /kənˌɡlɒməˈreɪʃn/ 33
consultation process
/ˌkɒnsəlˈteɪʃn ˈprəʊses/ 7
consumer demand
/kənˈsjuːmə dɪˈmɑːnd/ 11
consumer panels
/kənˈsjuːmə ˈpænlz/ 14
consumers /kənˈsjuːməz/ 6
contact points /ˈkɒntækt pɔɪnts/ 20
content related advertising
/ˈkɒntent rɪˈleɪtɪd ˈædvətaɪzɪŋ/ 15
contingency plan
/kənˈtɪndʒənsi plæn/ 17, 38
contingent reward leadership
/kənˈtɪndʒənt rɪˈwɔːd ˈliːdəʃɪp/ 27
continuous learning
/kənˈtɪnjʊəs ˈlɜːnɪŋ/ 26
contract of employment
/ˈkɒntrækt əv ɪmˈplɔɪmənt/ 22
contribution margin
/ˌkɒntrɪˈbjuːʃn ˈmɑːdʒɪn/ 29
contributory factors
/kənˈtrɪbjʊtəri ˈfæktəz/ 9
co-option /kəʊ ˈɒpʃn/ 39
coordination /kəʊˌɔːdɪnˈeɪʃn/ 38
copy-cat brand /ˈkɒpɪkæt brænd/ 12
copyright /ˈkɒpɪraɪt/ 10
copyright violations
/ˈkɒpɪraɪt ˌvaɪəˈleɪʃnz/ 10
core and non-core business
processes /kɔːr ənd ˈnɒnˈkɔː ˈbɪznəs ˈprəʊsesɪz/ 18
core competencies
/kɔː ˈkɒmpɪtənsiz/ 18,37
corporate culture
/ˈkɔːpərət ˈkʌltʃə/ 28
corporate governance
/ˈkɔːpərət ˈɡʌvənəns/ 34

corporate plan /ˈkɔːpərət plæn/ 38
corporate strategy
/ˈkɔːpərət ˈstrætədʒi/ 38
cost centre /kɒst ˈsentə/ 29
cost control /kɒst kənˈtrəʊl/ 29
cost forces /kɒst ˈfɔːsɪz/ 37
cost position /kɒst pəˈzɪʃn/ 37
court order /kɔːt ˈɔːdə/ 10
covenant /ˈkʌvənənt/ 31
cover costs /ˈkʌvə kɒsts/ 1
create strong bonds
/kriːˈeɪt strɒŋ bɒndz/ 27
create value /kriːˈeɪt ˈvælju/ 38
creative work /kriːˈeɪtɪv wɜːk/ 10
creativity /kriːeɪˈtɪvɪti/ 6
credit bureaux /ˈkredɪt ˈbjʊərəʊz/ 31
credit crunch /ˈkredɪt krʌntʃ/ 36
credit history /ˈkredɪt ˈhɪstri/ 31
credit rating /ˈkredɪt ˈreɪtɪŋ/ 31
credit score /ˈkredɪt skɔː/ 31
credit search /ˈkredɪt sɜːtʃ/ 31
credit transfer /ˈkredɪt ˈtrænsfɜː/ 31
creditors /ˈkredɪtəz/ 29
credits /ˈkredɪts/ 29
creditworthiness /ˈkredɪtwɜːðɪnəs/ 31
critical documents
/ˈkrɪtɪkl ˈdɒkjʊments/ 19
critical factors for success
/ˈkrɪtɪkl ˈfæktəz fə səkˈses/ 38
critical records /ˈkrɪtɪkl ˈrekɔːdz/ 19
cross-border mergers and
acquisitions /ˈkrɒˌsˌbɔːdə ˈmɜːdʒəz ənd ˌækwɪˈzɪʃnz/ 33
cross-cultural competences
/krɒs ˈkʌltʃərəl ˈkɒmpɪtənsɪz/ 28
cross-cultural differences
/krɒs ˈkʌltʃərəl ˈdɪfrənsɪz/ 28
cross-selling /krɒs ˈselɪŋ/ 20
cultural assumptions
/ˈkʌltʃərəl əˈsʌmpʃnz/ 28
cultural awareness
/ˈkʌltʃərəl əˈweənəs/ 28
cultural differences
/ˈkʌltʃərəl ˈdɪfrənsɪz/ 28
cultural diversity
/ˈkʌltʃərəl daɪˈvɜːsɪti/ 28
cultural impact
/ˈkʌltʃərəl ɪmˈpækt/ 28
cultural stereotypes
/ˈkʌltʃərəl ˈsterɪətaɪps/ 28
culture change /ˈkʌltʃə tʃeɪndʒ/ 20
culture shock /ˈkʌltʃə ʃɒk/ 28
current ratio /ˈkʌrənt ˈreɪʃɪəʊ/ 30
current trends /ˈkʌrənt trendz/ 38
customer base /ˈkʌstəmə beɪs/ 20
customer demand
/ˈkʌstəmə dɪˈmɑːnd/ 11
customer experience
/ˈkʌstəmər ɪkˈspɪərɪəns/ 20
customer focus /ˈkʌstəmə ˈfəʊkəs/ 11
customer journey mapping
/ˈkʌstəmə ˈdʒɜːni ˈmæpɪŋ/ 20

customer loyalty /ˈkʌstəmə ˈlɔɪəlti/ 13
customer needs /ˈkʌstəmə niːdz/ 12
customer perspective
/ˈkʌstəmə pəˈspektɪv/ 20
customer relationship management
/ˈkʌstəmə rɪˈleɪʃnʃɪp ˈmænɪdʒmənt/ 20
customer requirements
/ˈkʌstəmə rɪˈkwaɪəmənts/ 11
customer service /ˈkʌstəmə ˈsɜːvɪs/ 11
customers' stories
/ˈkəstəməz ˈstɔːriz/ 20
customer-facing /ˈkʌstəmə ˈfeɪsɪŋ/ 20
customer's specification
/ˈkəstəməz ˌspesɪfɪˈkeɪʃn/ 19
customized /ˈkʌstəmaɪzd/ 16
customized solutions
/ˈkəstəmaɪzdsəˈluːʃnz/ 31
daily rate /ˈdeɪli reɪt/ 5
data /ˈdeɪtə/ 5
data collection stage
/ˈdeɪtə kəˈlekʃn steɪdʒ/ 14
data mining /ˈdeɪtə ˈmaɪnɪŋ/ 5, 20
data security /ˈdeɪtə sɪˈkjʊərɪti/ 16
data warehousing
/ˈdeɪtə ˈweəhaʊzɪŋ/ 20
database /ˈdeɪtəbeɪs/ 5
day-release course
/deɪ rɪˈliːs kɔːs/ 24
deal with adversity
/diːl wɪð ədˈvɜːsəti/ 27
deal with conflict
/diːl wɪð kənˈflɪkt/ 1
deal with risk /diːl wɪð rɪsk/ 17
debits /ˈdebɪts/ 29
debt /det/ 30, 31
debt covenant /det ˈkʌvənənt/ 31
debt offering /det ˈɒfərɪŋ/ 32
debt to equity ratio
/det tu ˈekwɪti ˈreɪʃɪəʊ/ 32
decentralization
/ˌdiːsentrəlaɪzˈeɪʃn/ 3
decision gates /dɪˈsɪʒn geɪts/ 8
decision-making grid
/dəˈsɪʒnˌmekɪŋ grɪd/ 7
declining product
/dɪˈklaɪnɪŋ ˈprɒdʌkt/ 13
default /dɪˈfɔːlt/ 31
delegate /ˈdelɪgeɪt/ 28
deliver services /dɪˈlɪvə ˈsɜːvɪsɪz/ 13
delivered digitally
/dɪˈlɪvəd ˈdɪdʒɪtəli/ 16
depositors /dɪˈpɒzɪtəz/ 31
depreciation /dɪˌpriːʃɪˈeɪʃn/ 30
derivatives /dɪˈrɪvətɪvz/ 36
design /dɪˈzaɪn/ 9
design concept /dɪˈzaɪn ˈkɒnsept/ 6
design director /dɪˈzaɪn dɪˈrektə/ 9
determination /dɪˌtɜːmɪˈneɪʃn/ 25
develop creative thinking skills
/dɪˈveləp kriːˈeɪtɪv ˈθɪŋkɪŋ skɪlz/ 1

developing a prototype /dɪˈveləpɪŋ ə ˈprəʊtətaɪp/ 10

differentiate /ˌdɪfəˈrenʃieɪt/ 7, 37

diffuse /dɪˈfjuːz/ 9

digital downloads /ˈdɪdʒɪtl̩ ˌdaʊnˈləʊdz/ 15

digitally /ˈdɪdʒɪtəli/ 15

direct costs /dɪˈrekt kɒsts/ 29

direct debit /dɪˈrekt ˈdebɪt/ 31

directors /dɪˈrektəz/ 34

discount rate /ˈdɪskaʊnt reɪt/ 30

discounted cash flow /dɪsˈkaʊntɪd kæʃ fləʊ/ 30

discrimination /dɪˌskrɪmɪˈneɪʃn̩/ 22

discuss complex issues /dɪˈskʌs ˈkɒmpleks ˈɪʃuːz/ 1

discussion forum /dɪˈskʌʃn̩ ˈfɔːrəm/ 16, 21

dissatisfaction /dɪˈsætɪsfaɪd ˈkʌstəməz/ 23

distribute a product /dɪˈstrɪbjuːt ə ˈprɒdʌkt/ 13

distribution /ˌdɪstrɪˈbjuːʃn/ 7

diversification /daɪˌvɜːsɪfɪˈkeɪʃn/ 35

diversify /daɪˈvɜːsɪfaɪ/ 12

diversity /daɪˈvɜːsiti/ 22

dividends /ˈdɪvɪdendz/ 29

division of responsibilities /dɪˈvɪʒn̩ əv rɪˌspɒnsəˈbɪlɪtiz/ 34

documented procedures /ˈdɒkjʊmentɪd prəˈsiːdʒəz/ 19

donation /dəʊˈneɪʃn/ 4

double-loop learning /ˈdʌbl̩ luːp ˈlɜːnɪŋ/ 26

downloadable /daʊnˈləʊdəbl̩/ 15

draw up specifications /drɔː ʌp ˌspesɪfɪˈkeɪʃnz/ 18

dress code /dres kəʊd/ 28

driving forces /ˈdraɪvɪŋ ˈfɔːsɪz/ 39

due diligence /djuː ˈdɪlɪdʒəns/ 33

early adopters /ˈɜːli əˈdɒptəz/ 9

early majority /ˈɜːli məˈdʒɒrɪti/ 9

economies of scale /ɪˈkɒnəmiz əv skeɪl/ 21

effective communicator /ɪˈfektɪv kəˈmjuːnɪkeɪtə/ 1

e-learning /iː ˈlɜːnɪŋ/ 24

electronic transfer /ˌelekˈtrɒnɪk ˈtrænsfɜː/ 31

emergency planning officers /ɪˈmɜːdʒənsi ˈplænɪŋ ˈɒfɪsəz/ 17

emotional intelligence /ɪˈməʊʃnəl ɪnˈtelɪdʒəns/ 25

empathy /ˈempəθi/ 25

employment policies /ɪmˈplɔɪmənt ˈpɒləsiz/ 22

empowerment /ɪmˈpaʊəmənt/ 19, 40

encrypt /ɪnˈkrɪpt/ 21

ensure confidentiality /ɪnˈʃʊə ˌkɒnfɪˌdenʃɪˈælɪti/ 21

entrepreneur /ˌɒntrəprəˈnɜː/ 4

environmental factors /ɪnˌvaɪərənˈmentl̩ ˈfæktəz/ 38

environmentally friendly /ɪnˌvaɪərənˈmentəli ˈfrendli/ 11

equal access /ˈiːkwəl ˈækses/ 22

equal opportunities /ˈiːkwəl ˌɒpəˈtjuːnɪtiz/ 22

equal treatment /ˈiːkwəl ˈtriːtmənt/ 22

equality /ɪˈkwɒlɪti/ 22

equilibrium /ˌiːkwɪˈlɪbriəm/ 39

equity /ˈekwɪti/ 4, 32

equity buffers /ˈekwɪti ˈbʌfəz/ 36

equity financing /ˈekwɪti ˈfaɪnænsɪŋ/ 32

equity stake /ˈekwɪti steɪk/ 18, 29

establish the market /ɪˈstæblɪʃ ðə ˈmɑːkɪt/ 14

ethical investment /ˈeθɪkl̩ ɪnˈvestmənt/ 35

ethical values /ˈeθɪkl̩ ˈvæljuːz/ 12

evaluate /ɪˈvæljʊeɪt/ 9

evaluating the potential /ɪˈvæljʊeɪtɪŋ ðə pəˈtenʃl̩/ 7

exchange rate /ɪkˈstʃeɪndʒ reɪt/ 35

executive responsibility /ɪgˈzekjʊtɪv rɪˌspɒnsəˈbɪlɪti/ 34

executives /ɪgˈzekjʊtɪvz/ 34

existing firms /ɪgˈzɪstɪŋ fɜːmz/ 37

expand the range /ɪkˈspænd ðə reɪndʒ/ 12

expectations /ˌekspekˈteɪʃnz/ 19

explicit knowledge /ɪkˈsplɪsɪt ˈnɒlɪdʒ/ 26

export sales /ˈekspɔːt seɪlz/ 9

exposure /ɪkˈspəʊʒə/ 35

external auditors /ɪkˈstɜːnl̩ ˈɔːdɪtəz/ 34

external environment /ɪkˈstɜːnl̩ ɪnˈvaɪərənmənt/ 38

facilitator /fəˈsɪlɪteɪtə/ 24

fact-based decision making /fækt beɪst dɪˈsɪʒn̩ ˈmeɪkɪŋ/ 19

fair price /feə praɪs/ 30

fair value /feə ˈvæljuː/ 30

fairness /ˈfeənəs/ 27

FAQs /ˌefˌeɪˈkjuːz/ 21

feasibility /ˌfiːzəˈbɪlɪti/ 13

feasibility study /ˌfiːzəˈbɪlɪti ˈstʌdi/ 8

Federal Reserve /ˈfedərəl rɪˈzɜːv/ 36

feedback /ˈfiːdbæk/ 23

feel accountable /fiːl əˈkaʊntəbl̩/ 40

femininity /ˌfeməˈnɪnɪti/ 28

fiduciaries /fəˈduːʃiˌeriz/ 34

figurehead /ˈfɪɡəhed/ 1

financial accounting /faɪˈnænʃl̩ əˈkaʊntɪŋ/ 29

financial analysts /faɪˈnænʃl̩ ˈænəlɪsts/ 30

financial criteria /faɪˈnænʃl̩ kraɪˈtɪərɪə/ 7

financial ratio analysis /faɪˈnænʃl̩ ˈreɪʃəʊ əˈnæləsɪs/ 30

financial services /faɪˈnænʃl̩ ˈsɜːvɪsɪz/ 31

financial statements /faɪˈnænʃl̩ ˈsteɪtmənts/ 29

financial surplus /faɪˈnænʃl̩ ˈsɜːpləs/ 4

findings /ˈfaɪndɪŋz/ 14

finished goods /ˈfɪnɪʃt ɡʊdz/ 17

first tranche /fɜːst trɑːnʃ/ 32

fit for purpose /fɪt fə ˈpɜːpəs/ 18, 19

fixed costs /fɪkst kɒsts/ 29

flat structure /flæt ˈstrʌktʃə/ 2

flattened hierarchy /ˈflætn̩d ˈhaɪərɑːki/ 24

fast moving consumer goods /fɑːst ˈmuːvɪŋ kənˈsjuːmə ɡʊdz/ 11

focus groups /ˈfəʊkəs ɡruːps/ 8, 14

followers /ˈfɒləʊəz/ 27

force field analysis /fɔːs fiːld əˈnæləsɪs/ 39

force field diagram /fɔːs fiːld ˈdaɪəɡræm/ 39

forecasting techniques /ˈfɔːkɑːstɪŋ tekˈniːks/ 38

formal alliance /ˈfɔːml̩ əˈlaɪəns/ 18

forming /ˈfɔːmɪŋ/ 25

forward planning /ˈfɔːwəd ˈplænɪŋ/ 38

forward projections /ˈfɔːwəd prəˈdʒekʃnz/ 29

fostering self-development /ˈfɒstərɪŋ ˌselfdɪˈveləpmənt/ 27

fraud /frɔːd/ 31

free cash flows /friː kæʃ fləʊz/ 30

fully online /ˈfʊli ˌɒnˈlaɪn/ 16

functional departments /ˈfʌŋkʃnəl dɪˈpɑːtmənts/ 2

funding /ˈfʌndɪŋ/ 5

gap analysis /ɡæp əˈnæləsɪs/ 12

gate criteria /ɡeɪt kraɪˈtɪərɪə/ 8

generate a profit /ˈdʒenəreɪt ə ˈprɒfɪt/ 4

generic strategy /dʒɪˈnerɪk ˈstrætədʒi/ 37

geographical divisions /ˌdʒɪəˈɡræfɪkl̩ dɪˈvɪʒnz/ 2

gestures /ˈdʒestʃəz/ 28

get down to something /ɡet daʊn tu ˈsʌmθɪŋ/ 25

get on with someone /ɡet ɒn wɪð ˈsʌmwʌn/ 25

get the job done /ɡet ðə dʒɒb dʌn/ 25

get through /ɡet θruː/ 25

get to know someone /ɡet tu nəʊ ˈsʌmwʌn/ 25

global retailer /ˈɡləʊbl̩ ˈriːteɪlə/ 12

global risks /ˈɡləʊbl̩ rɪsks/ 17

go online /ɡəʊ ˌɒnˈlaɪn/ 15

go public /ɡəʊ ˈpʌblɪk/ 32

goal attainment /ɡəʊl əˈteɪnmənt/ 40

going concern /ˈɡəʊɪŋ kənˈsɜːn/ 30

government statistics /ˈɡʌvənmənt stəˈtɪstɪks/ 8

grade /ɡreɪd/ 5

grant copyright permissions /ɡrɑːnt ˈkɒpɪraɪt pəˈmɪʃnz/ 10

grants /ɡrɑːnts/ 5, 32

greater efficiency /ˈɡreɪtər ɪˈfɪʃnsi/ 3

green agenda /ɡriːn əˈdʒendə/ 14

gross margin /grəʊs ˈmɑːdʒɪn/ 29

gross profit margin / grəʊs ˈprɒfɪt ˈmɑːdʒɪn/ 30

group cohesion /gruːp kəʊˈhiːʒn̩/ 25

group norms /gruːp nɔːmz/ 25

group work /gruːp wɜːk/ 22

guidance notes /ˈgaɪdn̩s nəʊts/ 21

have a propensity to /həv ə prəˈpensiti tu/ 6

hedge fund /hedʒ fʌnd/ 35

hedging /ˈhedʒɪŋ/ 35

high flyers /haɪ ˈflaɪəz/ 26

high volume sales /haɪ ˈvɒljuːm seɪlz/ 37

highly successful business /ˈhaɪli səkˈsesfəl ˈbɪznəs/ 9

high-pressure sales approach /haɪ ˈpreʃə seɪlz əˈprəʊtʃ/ 11

hire /ˈhaɪə/ 22

historic cost /hɪˈstɒrɪk kɒst/ 30

holding stock /ˈhəʊldɪŋ stɒk/ 18

horizontal integration /ˌhɒrɪˈzɒntl̩ ˌɪntɪˈgreɪʃn/ 33

housing market /ˈhaʊzɪŋ ˈmɑːkɪt/ 36

human resources strategy /ˈhjuːmən rɪˈzɔːsɪz ˈstrætədʒi/ 22

hygiene factors /ˈhaɪdʒiːn ˈfæktəz/ 23

idealized influence /aɪˈdɪəlaɪzd ˈɪnfluəns/ 27

implemented /ˈɪmplɪmentɪd/ 19

inbound logistics /ˈɪnbaʊnd ləˈdʒɪstɪks/ 17

incentives /ɪnˈsentɪvz/ 34

incidental expenditure /ˌɪnsɪˈdentl̩ ɪkˈspendɪtʃə/ 5

income statement /ˈɪŋkʌm ˈsteɪtmənt/ 29

indirect costs /ˌɪndɪˈrekt kɒsts/ 29

individual consideration /ˌɪndɪˈvɪdʒuəl kənˌsɪdəˈreɪʃn/ 27

individualism /ˌɪndɪˈvɪdʒuəlɪzəm/ 28

induction programme /ɪnˈdʌkʃn ˈprəʊgræm/ 22

induction training /ɪnˈdʌkʃn ˈtreɪnɪŋ/ 24

industry bodies /ˈɪndəstri ˈbɒdiz/ 8

inertia /ɪˈnɜːʃə/ 39

ingenuity /ˌɪndʒɪˈnjuːɪti/ 6

in-house /ˈɪnˌhaʊs/ 17

in-house sources /ˈɪnˌhaʊs ˈsɔːsɪz/ 8

initial concept /ɪˈnɪʃl̩ ˈkɒnsept/ 6

initial exchanges /ɪˈnɪʃl̩ ɪkˈstʃeɪndʒɪz/ 25

initial order /ɪˈnɪʃl̩ ˈɔːdə/ 18

initial public offering (IPO) /ɪˈnɪʃl̩ ˈpʌblɪk ˈɒfərɪŋ (ˌaɪˈpiːˈəʊ)/ 32

innovate /ˈɪnəveɪt/ 6

innovation /ˌɪnəˈveɪʃn/ 6

innovative product /ˈɪnəveɪtɪv ˈprɒdʌkt/ 9

innovators /ˈɪnəveɪtəz/ 9

inside information /ɪnˈsaɪd ˌɪnfəˈmeɪʃn/ 34

inspirational motivation /ˌɪnspəˈreɪʃn̩əl ˌməʊtɪˈveɪʃn/ 27

institutional investor /ˌɪnstɪˈtjuːʃnəl ɪnˈvestə/ 4

institutional shareholder /ˌɪnstɪˈtjuːʃnəl ˈʃeəhəʊldə/ 4

intangible services /ɪnˈtændʒəbl̩ ˈsɜːvɪsɪz/ 13

integrate /ˈɪntɪgreɪt/ 1

integrity /ɪnˈtegrɪti/ 27

intellectual capital /ˌɪntəˈlektʃuəl ˈkæpɪtəl/ 26

intellectual property /ˌɪntəˈlektʃuəl ˈprɒpəti/ 10

intellectual stimulation /ˌɪntəˈlektʃuəl ˌstɪmjuˈleɪʃn/ 27

interact with clients /ˌɪntəˈrækt wɪð ˈklaɪənts/ 1

interactive features /ˌɪntəˈræktɪv ˈfiːtʃəz/ 16

interbank lending rates /ˌɪntərˈbæŋk ˈlendɪŋ reɪts/ 36

interest rate /ˈɪntrəst reɪt/ 31

internal audit /ɪnˈtɜːnl̩ ˈɔːdɪt/ 19

internal customers /ɪnˈtɜːnl̩ ˈkʌstəməz/ 24

internal environment /ɪnˈtɜːnl̩ ɪnˈvaɪərənmənt/ 38

internal performance /ɪnˈtɜːnl̩ pəˈfɔːməns/ 12

internal supply chain /ɪnˈtɜːnl̩ səˈplaɪ tʃeɪn/ 19

interpersonal relationships /ˌɪntəˈpɜːsənl rɪˈleɪʃnʃɪps/ 23, 25

invention /ɪnˈvenʃn/ 6

inventory /ˈɪnvəntri/ 21

inventory control /ˈɪnvəntri kənˈtrəʊl/ 5

inventory management system /ˈɪnvəntri ˈmænɪdʒmənt ˈsɪstəm/ 21

investment bank /ɪnˈvestmənt bæŋk/ 32

investment portfolio /ɪnˈvestmənt pɔːtˈfəʊliəʊ/ 35

investment vehicle /ɪnˈvestmənt ˈviːɪkl̩/ 35

invoice /ˈɪnvɔɪs/ 5

Islamic banking /ɪzˈlæmɪk bæŋkɪŋ/ 35

job advertisement /dʒɒb ədˈvɜːtɪsmənt/ 22

job description /dʒɒb dɪˈskrɪpʃn/ 22

job enlargement /dʒɒb ɪnˈlɑːdʒmənt/ 23

job enrichment /dʒɒb ɪnˈrɪtʃmənt/ 23

job rotation /dʒɒb rəʊˈteɪʃn/ 23

job satisfaction /dʒɒb ˌsætɪsˈfækʃn/ 23

job security /dʒɒb sɪˈkjʊərɪti/ 23

joint venture /dʒɔɪnt ˈventʃə/ 33

junior consultant /ˈdʒuːnɪə kənˈsʌltənt/ 5

just-in-time /dʒʌst ɪn taɪm/ 21

key criteria /kiː kraɪˈtɪərɪə/ 7

key performance indicators /kiː pəˈfɔːməns ˈɪndɪkeɪtəz/ 1

key players /kiː ˈpleɪəz/ 39

killer idea /ˈkɪlər aɪˈdɪə/ 10

knowledge management /ˈnɒlɪdʒ ˈmænɪdʒmənt/ 26

knowledge networking /ˈnɒlɪdʒ netwɜːkɪŋ/ 26

knowledge working /ˈnɒlɪdʒ ˈwɜːkɪŋ/ 3

laggards /ˈlægədz/ 9

laissez-faire approach /ˌleɪseɪ ˈfeər əˈprəʊtʃ/ 27

late majority /leɪt məˈdʒɒrɪti/ 9

launch /lɔːntʃ/ 6

layers of management /ˈleɪəz əv ˈmænɪdʒmənt/ 2

lead users /liːd ˈjuːzəz/ 6

leadership /ˈliːdəʃɪp/ 1, 27

leadership qualities /ˈliːdəʃɪp ˈkwɒlɪtiz/ 27

learning organization /ˈlɜːnɪŋ ˌɔːgənəˈzeɪʃn/ 26

legal entity /ˈliːgl̩ ˈentɪti/ 34

legal sharing /ˈliːgl̩ ˈʃeərɪŋ/ 10

legally binding contract /ˈliːgəli ˈbaɪndɪŋ ˈkɒntrækt/ 18

legislation /ˌledʒɪsˈleɪʃn/ 14

legitimate /lɪˈdʒɪtɪmət/ 10

lend money /lend ˈmʌni/ 31

lending criteria /ˈlendɪŋ kraɪˈtɪərɪə/ 31

levels of service /ˈlevlz əv ˈsɜːvɪs/ 20

leveraged /ˈliːvərɪdʒd/ 36

liabilities /ˌlaɪəˈbɪlɪtiz/ 29

liability /ˌlaɪəˈbɪlɪti/ 34

liaising with /liˈeɪzɪŋ wɪð/ 1

lifespan /ˈlaɪfspæn/ 13

likely customers /ˈlaɪkli ˈkʌstəməz/ 14

line manager /laɪn ˈmænɪdʒə/ 24

lines of responsibility /laɪnz əv rɪˌspɒnsəˈbɪlɪti/ 2

loan application /ləʊn ˌæplɪˈkeɪʃn/ 31

loans /ləʊnz/ 5

logistics /ləˈdʒɪstɪks/ 5, 17

long-term solvency /lɒŋ tɜːm ˈsɒlvənsi/ 30

loyal to brands /ˈlɔɪəl tu brændz/ 20

macro environment /ˈmækrəʊ ɪnˈvaɪərənmənt/ 3

maintain the status quo /meɪnˈteɪn ðə ˈsteɪtəs ˈkwəʊ/ 39

make a profit /meɪk ə ˈprɒfɪt/ 1

manage conflict /ˈmænɪdʒ ˈkɒnflɪkt/ 27

management discipline /ˈmænɪdʒmənt ˈdɪsɪplɪn/ 11

management instrument /ˈmænɪdʒmənt ˈɪnstrəmənt/ 14

management accounting /ˈmænɪdʒmənt əˈkaʊntɪŋ/ 29

management by objectives /ˈmænɪdʒmənt baɪ əbˈdʒektɪvz/ 3

peers /pɪəz/ 23
pension fund /ˈpenʃn fʌnd/ 35
performance appraisal
  /pəˈfɔːməns əˈpreɪzl/ 24
performance milestones
  /pəˈfɔːməns ˈmaɪlstəʊnz/ 32
performed poorly /pəˈfɔːmd
  ˈpʊəli/ 25
period of conflict
  /ˈpɪərɪəd əv ˈkɒnflɪkt/ 25
permanent posts
  /ˈpɜːmənənt pəʊsts/ 22
personality traits
  /ˌpɜːsəˈnælɪti treɪts/ 27
personality types /
  ˌpɜːsəˈnælɪti taɪps/ 25
personalized lists
  /ˌpɜːsənlˌaɪzd lɪsts/ 16
physical outlets /ˈfɪzɪkl ˈaʊtlets/ 16
planning and scheduling
  /ˈplænɪŋ ənd ˈʃedjuːlɪŋ/ 4
plausible hypothesis
  /ˈplɔːzəbl haɪˈpɒθəsɪs/ 38
podcast /ˈpɒdkaːst/ 15
portfolios /pɔːtˈfəʊliəʊz/ 35
positioning themselves
  /pəˈzɪʃnɪŋ ðəmˈselvz/ 37
positive cash flow
  /ˈpɒzətɪv kæʃ fləʊ/ 29
post-merger integration
  /pəʊst ˈmɜːdʒə ˌɪntɪˈgreɪʃn/ 33
potential customers
  /pəˈtenʃl ˈkʌstəməz/ 6
potential risks /pəˈtenʃl rɪsks/ 17
power distance /ˈpaʊə ˈdɪstəns/ 28
predictions /prɪˈdɪkʃnz/ 38
pre-employment checks
  /priːmˈplɔɪmənt tʃeks/ 22
premises /ˈpremɪsɪz/ 13
premium /ˈpriːmɪəm/ 33
premium services
  /ˈpriːmɪəm ˈsɜːvɪsɪz/ 15
pressures for change
  /ˈpreʃəz fə tʃeɪndʒ/ 39
pre-technical evaluation
  /priːˈteknɪkl ɪˌvæljuˈeɪʃn/ 8
pre-tender queries
  /priːˈtendə ˈkwɪəriz/ 21
prevailing culture
  /prɪˈveɪlɪŋ ˈkʌltʃə/ 28
price /praɪs/ 13
price-comparison websites
  /praɪs kəmˈpærɪsn ˈwebsaɪts/ 16
price-earnings ratio
  /praɪs ˈɜːnɪŋz ˈreɪʃɪəʊ/ 30
primary activities
  /ˈpraɪməri ækˈtɪvətiz/ 17
primary market research
  /ˈpraɪməri ˈmaːkɪt rɪˈsɜːtʃ/ 8, 11
principal /ˈprɪnsəpl/ 34
principal-agency problem
  /ˈprɪnsəpl ˈeɪdʒənsi
  ˈprɒbləm/ 34
principles of Taylorism
  /ˈprɪnsəplz əv teɪlərɪzm/ 3
prioritize risks /praɪˈɒrɪtaɪz
  rɪsks/ 17

private limited company
  /ˈpraɪvɪt ˈlɪmɪtɪd ˈkʌmpəni/ 34
private ownership
  /ˈpraɪvɪt ˈəʊnəʃɪp/ 4
private venture capital partnerships
  /ˈpraɪvɪt ˈventʃə ˈkæpɪtəl
  ˈpaːtnəʃɪps/ 32
processes /ˈprəʊsesɪz/ 3, 17
procurement /prəˈkjʊəmənt/ 17
procurement budget
  /prəˈkjʊəmənt ˈbʌdʒət/ 21
procurement department
  /prəˈkjʊəmənt dɪˈpaːtmənt/ 18
product awareness
  /ˈprɒdʌkt əˈweənəs/ 13
product champions
  /ˈprɒdʌkt ˈtʃæmpɪənz/ 8, 16
product criteria
  /ˈprɒdʌkt kraɪˈtɪərɪə/ 7
product development
  /ˈprɒdʌkt dɪˈveləpmənt/ 6
product divisions
  /ˈprɒdʌkt dɪˈvɪʒnz/ 2
product-extension merger
  /ˈprɒdʌkt ɪkˈstenʃn
  ˈmɜːdʒə/ 33
product launch /ˈprɒdʌkt lɔːntʃ/ 8
product life cycle
  /ˈprɒdʌkt laɪf ˈsaɪkl/ 8, 13
product portfolio
  /ˈprɒdʌkt pɔːtˈfəʊlɪəʊ/ 7
production process
  /prəˈdʌkʃn ˈprəʊses/ 3
production targets
  /prəˈdʌkʃn ˈtaːgɪts/ 3
production-led /prəˈdʌkʃn led/ 11
productivity rates
  /ˌprɒdʌkˈtɪvɪti reɪts/ 3
profit and loss account
  /ˈprɒfɪt ənd lɒs əˈkaʊnt/ 29
profit centre /ˈprɒfɪt ˈsentə/ 29
profit seeking /ˈprɒfɪt ˈsiːkɪŋ/ 4
profitability /ˌprɒfɪtˈəbl/ 30
project manager
  /prəˈdʒekt ˈmænɪdʒə/ 5
projected break-even point
  /prəˈdʒektɪd ˈbreɪˌkiːvən pɔɪnt/ 9
projected cash flows
  /prəˈdʒektɪd kæʃ fləʊz/ 32
promote teamwork
  /prəˈməʊt ˈtiːmwɜːk/ 25
promotion /prəˈməʊʃn/ 7, 13
promotional material
  /prəˈməʊʃnəl məˈtɪərɪəl/ 11
proprietary software
  /prəˈpraɪətri ˈsɒftweə/ 5
prospective suppliers
  /prəˈspektɪv səˈplaɪəz/ 21
prototype /ˈprəʊtətaɪp/ 6, 10
public limited company (plc)
  /ˈpʌblɪk ˈlɪmɪtɪd ˈkʌmpəni
  (ˌpiːˌelˈsiː)/ 34
public sector /ˈpʌblɪk ˈsektə/ 3
punctuality /ˌpʌŋktʃuˈælɪti/ 28
purchasing habits
  /ˈpɜːtʃəsɪŋ ˈhæbɪts/ 20
put in a tender /pʊt ɪn ə ˈtendə/ 21

qualified opinion
  /ˈkwɒlɪfaɪd əˈpɪnɪən/ 34
qualitative analysis
  /ˈkwɒlɪtətɪv əˈnæləsɪs/ 14
qualitative data /ˈkwɒlɪtətɪv
  ˈdeɪtə/ 8
quality assurance
  /ˈkwɒlɪti əˈʃɔːrəns/ 19
quality culture /ˈkwɒlɪti ˈkʌltʃə/ 19
quality management
  /ˈkwɒlɪti ˈmænɪdʒmənt/ 17
quality management system
  /ˈkwɒlɪti ˈmænɪdʒmənt
  ˈsɪstəm/ 19
quantitative analysis
  /ˈkwɒntɪtətɪv əˈnæləsɪs/ 14
quantitative data
  /ˈkwɒntɪtətɪv ˈdeɪtə/ 8
quantitative easing
  /ˈkwɒntɪtətɪv ˈiːzɪŋ/ 36
rate /reɪt/ 5
raw data /rɔː ˈdeɪtə/ 5
raw materials /rɔː məˈtɪərɪəlz/ 14
real cost /rɪəl kɒst/ 29
re-brand /riːbrænd/ 33
recession /rɪˈseʃn/ 36
recognition of achievement
  /ˌrekəgˈnɪʃn əv əˈtʃiːvmənt/ 23
recruit a new customer
  /rɪˈkruːt ə njuː ˈkʌstəmə/ 20
recruitment and selection
  process /rɪˈkruːtmənt
  ənd sɪˈlekʃn ˈprəʊses/ 22
red tape /red teɪp/ 23
redesign /ˌriːdɪˈzaɪn/ 9
referees /ˌrefəˈriːz/ 22
registered users /ˈredʒɪstəd
  ˈjuːzəz/ 21
regulated company
  /ˈregjʊleɪtɪd ˈkʌmpəni/ 35
regulation /ˌregjʊˈleɪʃn/ 36
remuneration /rɪˌmjuːnəˈreɪʃn/ 34
reorder levels /ˌriːˈɔːdə ˈlevlz/ 21
repayment schedule
  /rɪˈpeɪmənt ˈʃedjuːl/ 31
repeat purchases /rɪˈpiːt
  ˈpɜːtʃəsɪz/ 18
report on results
  /rɪˈpɔːt ɒn rɪˈzʌlts/ 1
research and development (R & D)
  /rɪˈsɜːtʃ ənd dɪˈveləpmənt
  (ˌaːrənˈdiː)/ 6, 13
research brief /rɪˈsɜːtʃ briːf/ 14
research expertise
  /rɪˈsɜːtʃ ˌekspɜːˈtiːz/ 26
reserves of currency
  /rɪˈzɜːvz əv ˈkʌrənsi/ 35
resistance to change
  /rɪˈzɪstəns tu tʃeɪndʒ/ 39
resisters /rɪˈzɪstəz/ 39
resource requirements
  /rɪˈzɔːs rɪˈkwaɪəmənts/ 12
resources /rɪˈzɔːsɪz/ 4, 27
respect for confidentiality
  /rɪˈspekt fə ˌkɒnfɪˌdenʃɪˈælɪti/ 24
restraining forces
  /rɪˈstreɪnɪŋ ˈfɔːsɪz/ 39

substitute product /ˈsʌbstɪtjuːt ˈprɒdʌkt/ 37
substitute services /ˈsʌbstɪtjuːt ˈsɜːvɪsɪz/ 37
suitably equipped /ˈsuːtəbli ɪˈkwɪpt/ 27
supplier /səˈplaɪə/ 18
supplier audit /səˈplaɪər ˈɔːdɪt/ 18
supply chain /səˈplaɪ tʃeɪn/ 17,18
supply chain management /səˈplaɪ tʃeɪn ˈmænɪdʒmənt/ 18
supply of goods /səˈplaɪ əv gʊdz/ 11
support activities /səˈpɔːt ækˈtɪvətiz/ 17
surplus funds /ˈsɜːpləs fʌndz/ 31
sustainability /səˈsteɪnəbḷ/ 14
sustainable business /səˈsteɪnəbḷ ˈbɪznəs/ 4
sustainable excellence /səˈsteɪnəbḷ ˈeksələns/ 19
SWIFT /swɪft/ 31
SWOT analysis /swɒt əˈnæləsɪs/ 12
synergy /ˈsɪnədʒi/ 33
tacit knowledge /ˈtæsɪt ˈnɒlɪdʒ/ 26
tactical plan /ˈtæktɪkḷ plæn/ 38
take charge of /teɪk tʃɑːdʒ ɒv/ 23
take out a patent /teɪk aʊt ə ˈpeɪtṇt/ 10
take remedial steps /teɪk rɪˈmiːdɪəl steps/ 18
take risks /teɪk rɪsks/ 6,27
takeover /ˈteɪkəʊvə/ 33
talent management and retention scheme / ˈtælənt ˈmænɪdʒmənt ənd rɪˈtenʃṇ skiːm/ 26
tall structure /tɔːl ˈstrʌktʃə/ 2
tangible and intangible benefits /ˈtændʒəbḷ ənd ɪnˈtændʒəbḷ ˈbenɪfɪts/ 35
tangible products /ˈtændʒəbḷ ˈprɒdʌkts/ 11, 13
tangibles /ˈtændʒəbəlz/ 13
target audience /ˈtɑːgɪt ˈɔːdiəns/ 16
tax-deductible /tæks dɪˈdʌktəbḷ/ 32
team appraisal /tiːm əˈpreɪzḷ/ 24
team development /tiːm dɪˈveləpmənt/ 25
team player /tiːm ˈpleɪə/ 1
team spirit /tiːm ˈspɪrɪt/ 25
teamworking /tiːmˈwɜːkɪŋ/ 25
teambuilding activities /ˈtiːmbɪldɪŋækˈtɪvətiz/ 27
technical development /ˈteknɪkḷ dɪˈveləpmənt/ 8
technical proposal /ˈteknɪkḷ prəˈpəʊzḷ/ 6
technical requirements /ˈteknɪkḷ rɪˈkwaɪəmənts/ 8
technical skills /ˈteknɪkḷ skɪlz/ 26
temporary contract /ˈtempri ˈkɒntrækt/ 22
tender /ˈtendə/ 21

tender documents /ˈtendə ˈdɒkjuments/ 21
terms of reference /tɜːmz əv ˈrefrəns/ 5
the 'great man' theory /ðə greɪt mæn ˈθɪəri/ 27
the board of directors /ðə bɔːd əv dɪˈrektəz/ 34
the commons /ðə ˈkɒmənz/ 10
the Companies Act /ðə ˈkʌmpəniz ækt/ 34
the customer rules /ðə ˈkʌstəmə ruːlz/ 19
theft /θeft/ 10
threatening /ˈθretṇɪŋ/ 24
time management software /taɪm ˈmænɪdʒmənt ˈsɒftweə/ 5
time value of money /taɪm ˈvæljuː əv ˈmʌni/ 30
timeframe /ˈtaɪmˌfreɪm/ 38
to be stretched /tu bi stretʃt/ 26
to evaluate a tender /tu ɪˈvæljʊeɪt ə ˈtendə/ 21
to get closer to their customers /tu get ˈkləʊsə tu ðeə ˈkʌstəməz/ 20
to have potential /tu həv pəˈtenʃḷ/ 12
to put out to tender /tu pʊt aʊt tu ˈtendə/ 21
too big to fail /tuː bɪg tu feɪl/ 36
toughness /ˈtʌfnəs/ 25
toxic assets /ˈtɒksɪk ˈæsets/ 36
tracking /ˈtrækɪŋ/ 20
trade directories /treɪd dɪˈrektəriz/ 18
trade off /treɪd ɒf/ 32
trade unions /treɪd ˈjuːnɪənz/ 14
trademarks /ˈtreɪdmɑːks/ 10
traditional advertising media /trəˈdɪʃnəl ˈædvətaɪzɪŋ ˈmiːdɪə/ 16
traditional design /trəˈdɪʃnəl dɪˈzaɪn/ 9
traditional methods /trəˈdɪʃnəl ˈmeθədz/ 15
training evaluation /ˈtreɪnɪŋ ɪˌvæljuˈeɪʃn/ 24
transaction /trænˈzækʃn/ 5
transactional leadership /trænˈzækʃnəl ˈliːdəʃɪp/ 27
transformational approach /ˌtrænsfəˈmeɪʃnəl əˈprəʊtʃ/ 33
transformational leadership /ˌtrænsfəˈmeɪʃnəl ˈliːdəʃɪp/ 27
transition period /trænˈzɪʃn ˈpɪərɪəd/ 39
transparency /trænsˈpærənsi/ 34
treasury department /ˈtreʒəri dɪˈpɑːtmənt/ 35
trendsetters /ˈtrendsetəz/ 16
trickle down /ˈtrɪkḷ daʊn/ 40
triple bottom line /ˈtrɪpḷ ˈbɒtəm laɪn/ 4
uncertainty avoidance /ʌnˈsɜːtṇti əˈvɔɪdəns/ 28

under a licence /ˈʌndər ə ˈlaɪsṇs/ 10
underlying assumptions /ˌʌndəˈlaɪɪŋ əˈsʌmpʃṇz/ 12
underwrite /ˌʌndəˈraɪt/ 36
unique product characteristics /juːˈniːk ˈprɒdʌkt ˌkærəktəˈrɪstɪks/ 7
unique selling point /juːˈniːk ˈselɪŋ pɔɪnt/ 32
unqualified opinion /ʌnˈkwɒlɪfaɪd əˈpɪnɪən/ 34
unwritten rules /ˌʌnˈrɪtṇ ruːlz/ 28
upward feedback /ˈʌpwəd ˈfiːdbæk/ 24
user-friendly /juːsəˈfrendli/ 21
valid concerns /ˈvælɪd kənˈsɜːnz/ 39
value analysis /ˈvæljuː əˈnæləsɪs/ 18
value chain /ˈvæljuː tʃeɪn/ 17
value proposition /ˈvæljuː ˌprɒpəˈzɪʃn/ 32
values /ˈvæljuːz/ 28
variable costs /ˈveərɪəbḷ kɒsts/ 29
variables /ˈveərɪəbḷz/ 39
vendor /ˈvendə/ 18
venture capital /ˈventʃə ˈkæpɪtəl/ 32
venture capitalists /ˈventʃə ˈkæpɪtəlɪsts/ 5, 32
vertical integration /ˈvɜːtɪkḷ ˌɪntɪˈgreɪʃn/ 33
vested interests /ˈvestɪd ˈɪntrəsts/ 39
viability /ˌvaɪəˈbɪlɪti/ 6
viral marketing /ˈvaɪrəl ˈmɑːkɪtɪŋ/ 16
virtual team /ˈvɜːtʃʊəl tiːm/ 24
vision /ˈvɪʒn/ 9
vision statement /ˈvɪʒṇ ˈsteɪtmənt/ 40
volatile /ˈvɒlətaɪl/ 35
volunteers /ˌvɒlənˈtɪəz/ 4
vulnerable /ˈvʌlnərəbḷ/ 17
waged /weɪdʒd/ 4
waive competition law /weɪv ˌkɒmpəˈtɪʃn lɔː/ 36
Wall Street /wɔːl striːt/ 36
waste material /weɪst məˈtɪərɪəl/ 14
well-balanced team /wel ˈbælənst tiːm/ 27
well-being /wel ˈbiːɪŋ/ 23
what if /wɒt ɪf/ 38
white goods /waɪt gʊdz/ 11
wide variety of skills /waɪd vəˈraɪəti əv skɪlz/ 23
work off-site /wɜːk ɒf saɪt/ 5
workforce /ˈwɜːkfɔːs/ 22
working capital ratio /ˈwɜːkɪŋ ˈkæpɪtəl ˈreɪʃɪəʊ/ 30
working conditions /ˈwɜːkɪŋ kənˈdɪʃnz/ 23
work shadowing /ˈwɜːk ʃædəʊɪŋ/ 24

Acknowledgements

The authors and publishers acknowledge the following sources of copyright material and are grateful for the permissions granted. While every effort has been made, it has not always been possible to identify the sources of all the material used, or to trace all copyright holders. If any omissions are brought to our notice, we will be happy to include the appropriate acknowledgements on reprinting.

Photograph on page 12, Lukasz Bizon / Shutterstock.com; photograph on page 18, NRT-Helena / Alamy; Tony Hsieh for the text on page 21; Amazon for the adapted text on page 29; text on page 41, exercise 17.3 is adapted from *Management Standards*, 2004; photograph on page 24, Kalulu / iStock; photo on page 40, Stockbyte; text on page 42, section A is adapted from *The Economist: Guide to Management Ideas and Gurus*, Economist Books, 2008; text on page 43, exercise 18.3 on page 43 is *adapted from* www.peoplemanagement.co.uk the online magazine of The Chartered Institute of Personnel and Development; section C on page 44 is based on detail of the EFQM Excellence Model published online at www.efqm.org (last accessed August 2011); exercise 19.3 on page 45 uses text from the ISO website www.iso.org (last accessed July 2011); the Cameroon document on page 48 is adapted from material by UK Trade and Investment; photograph on page 66, jvoisey / iStock; Financial Times Ltd. for the text on page 68 on cash management, adapted from www.thebanker.com; UK Financial Reporting Council for the text on the board of directors on page 74; photograph on page 76, Gordon Heeley / iStock; McKinsey & Company for the Heat Map reproduced on page 77, © McKinsey & Company; the text in sections A and B on page 78 is adapted from *The Guardian* article "Three weeks that changed the world" published 28 December 2008, the text in section B on that page further sources from *The Economist* article "Buffer warren" published 29 October 2008 and from the www.financemarkets.co.uk article "Libor rate rise threatens banking system" published 16 September 2008; the diagram on page 80 is reproduced with permission of Free Press, a division of Simon & Schuster, Inc. from *Competitive Strategy: Techniques for Analyzing Industries and Competitors* by Michael E. Porter, © 1980 Free Press; the diagram on page 84 is adapted from *Management: A Pacific Rim Focus* by K. Bartol, M. Tein, G. Matthews and D. Martin with permission from McGraw Hill; diagram on page 86 from www.mindtools.com; © Mind Tools Ltd., with permission; Cambridge University Press for definition in answer to exercise 21.2, page 103, sourced from Cambridge Advanced Learners' Dictionary.